Reading
Between
the Lines

Reading
Between
the Lines

*Discovering the One Purpose Behind
the Twenty-seven Books of the New Testament*

ALGER FITCH

 COLLEGE PRESS
PUBLISHING COMPANY
Joplin, Missouri

Library of Congress Cataloging-in-Publication Data

Fitch, Alger Morton
    Reading between the lines: discovering the one purpose
behind the twenty-seven books of the New Testament /
Alger Fitch.
      p.   cm.
    Includes bibliographical references (p. 191).
    ISBN 0-89900-733-3
    1. Bible. N.T.—Criticism, interpretation, etc. 2. Bible,
N.T.—Inspiration. I. Title
    BS2361.F6 1995
    225.6—dc20   95-24560
                                         CIP

Contents

Preface

"From God to man with love" are words that could be attached to each of the manuscripts that make up our New Testament. The twenty-seven "love letters" that we call the New Testament reveal heaven's reach for the people of earth.

This overview of the New Covenant writings — *The New Testament on Purpose* — finds the winning of the world the target toward which each separate arrow is aimed. Like other introductions to the Gospels, Epistles and Revelation, this study will consider the who, where, when and what questions. But the difference will be the emphasis on the priority query, "Why?"

The Bible reader is most apt to discover the scriptural penman's meaning when he or she recognizes the driving force that was in the writer's soul and the controlling factor that stimulated the author to put on paper what he did. The reason — the purpose — the why — is "of first importance" (1 Cor. 15:3).

This survey is not intended to be a technical work to challenge the specialist's views on every issue and problem. That would possibly confuse the lowly sheep who need feeding, more than it would stretch the neck of the curious giraffes. At the same time, this work is not simply another devotional overview to inspire one's feelings, yet fail to guide the believer to make Jesus' last command his first concern.

In the following pages I want you to consider the Gospels as missionary sermons (Part I), the Acts as missionary records (Part II), the Epistles as missionary correspondence (Part III) and the Revelation as missionary struggles (Part IV). I pray that you will come to see the New Testament and the Great Commission as identical twins. It is my conviction that, if the Risen Christ had not placed in His followers a missionary concern, there would have been no New Testament. Consider your Bible as if it were a pair of binoculars or a telescope. For too long we have looked *at* what was intended to be looked *through*. To look beyond the words on the page to the human author's purpose, to look all the way to the Divine Author's heart, is to see the Almighty longing to redeem all the creatures made in His image.

"It's all in the way you look at it!" That remark is true. So look at your Bible from the missionary perspective. It will do you good. It will do a congregation good. Consider it God's Book for His global mission. This concept is no novel view. W.O. Carver in *Missions in the Plan of the Ages* stated that the New Testament "is first of all, a product of the missionary work of the early Christians, and it was produced primarily to meet the needs of this work."[1] James Moffatt, in an article on "The Formation of the New Testament," reflected, "Probably there is no New Testament book written directly for outsiders, but every book was written more or less for communities which were conscious of their responsibility for the great mission and of their witness in the enterprise."[2]

To read the New Testament, aware that every part was written by a missionary to a newly founded church or to the convert of a missionary, ought to take the missionary task from the hands of a single worker on foreign soil, or a small committee in a local church, and place it on every Bible

---

[1] W.O. Carver, *Missions in the Plan of the Ages* (Nashville: Broadman Press), pp. 22-23.

[2] *The Abingdon Bible Commentary* (New York: The Abingdon Press, 1929), p. 859.

reader's heart where it belongs. To remember that the original writers wrote in *Koine* Greek — the international language — rather than a particular dialect known only in one area, bares the writer's missionary interest to reach every people. Also to recall that every translation today into the multitude of present dialects, makes evident that the modern church has not forgotten its focus on winning those of "every nation, tribe, people and language" (Rev. 7:9).

May the Holy Spirit, who inspired those original authors of the New Testament in the First Century, inspire us to keep on the same soul-winning course as we prepare to enter the Twenty-first Century. May it please the Savior of the millions who are today "in Christ," to recommit His disciples to His commission to reach the over three billion still "out of Christ." May the Eternal Father who yearns for the return of each Prodigal, stimulate in us who read the New Testament an unquenchable longing to put our focus where He has His.

Dietrich Bonhoeffer was never more right than when he stated, "The Church is the Church only when it exists for others."[3] World evangelism is the most basic of the basics — the most fundamental of the fundamentals. What every Christian must know about the church, above what past history and present experiences teach, is what Christ means His church to be. That is found both in the lines — and between the lines — written by the New Testament authors.

---

[3]Dietrich Bonhoeffer, *Letters and Papers from Prison* (New York: Macmillan, 1953), p. 203.

Old Testament Anticipation

The Christian's Bible contains both an Old Testament and a New Testament. In the words of Thomas Watson, "The two Testaments are the two lips by which God has spoken to us." All the Scripture's 31,173 verses and over 773,000 words communicate to the reader an awareness that God is on a mission to reach mankind.

While the book you are now reading will concentrate on the New Testament evidence of that Divine love, we begin with the affirmation that from cover to cover the Old Testament anticipated world missions. The man that historians have called Saint Ambrose noted that God walks in the Holy Scriptures seeking man today as Genesis says He did in Paradise.

Listen to the Law About World Outreach

As the opening book of the New Testament introduces us to Jesus Christ who died for all and sent forth proclaimers to speak the message to all, the lead book of the Old Testament presents the God who made us all. This God, revealing Himself and His purposes, is no minor deity ruling over some small river, high hill or single clan. He is rather the One who "in the beginning . . . created the heavens and the earth" (Gen. 1:1; 2:4; 5:1-2; 14:19) and made mankind to "rule . . . over all the earth" (1:26) and to "fill the earth" (1:28). Adam, the first man, and Eve, "the mother of all the living" (3:20), became the first sinners. At this point, the redemption story begins to unfold that, He who made us all and finds sin affecting us all, offers hope to us all because of His grace.

The universality of sin makes evident the universal need for forgiveness. The God of compassion chose Abram to begin the lineage for the Messiah, stating, "All peoples on earth will be blessed through you" (12:3). He later added, "All nations on earth will be blessed" (22:18). Please note that the God of the Old Testament has His eye on "all nations." The Jewish nation, rising through Abraham, Isaac and Jacob, was to be the "chosen people" in the sense of being God's instrument in bringing the knowledge of the Creator to the entire world.

The Torah of Moses, that stands first in the Judeo-Christian Scriptures, acknowledges one God and He is "the God of earth" (24:3). No tribal deity is He. Hezekiah later prayed: "O LORD, God of Israel . . . you alone are God over all the kingdoms of the earth. You have made heaven and earth" (2 Kings 19:15). The Bible's God is world-creating and all-earth caring. David understood Israel's mission to all peoples, when he taught Asaph and his associates to sing, "Give thanks to the LORD, call on his name; make known among the nations what he has done. . . . Declare his glory among the nations, his marvelous deeds among all peoples" (1 Chron. 16:8,24).

Be Helped by the Hymns About World Outreach

The 150 Psalms sung by the people of the Torah join in their praise of the God of all the nations. The theology of any religious group will be reflected in the songs they sing.

Thumb through the Jewish hymnal, known as the Book of Psalms. Listen for the recurring refrain of God's awareness of the whole world and His concern for every person.

Psalm 2 is the Messianic Psalm in which the Lord speaks: "You are my Son" (2:7) and promises, "I will make the nations your inheritance, the ends of the earth your possession" (2:8). Psalm 8 sings out that the LORD's name is "majestic . . . in all the earth!" (8:1,9). The next Psalm calls on the worshiper to not only praise God in Zion, but also to "proclaim among the nations what he has done" (9:11). That the Heavenly Father should be praised "among the nations" is the crescendo in 18:49, 108:3 and 117:1. There in full volume the choir refers again to "all you nations . . . all you peoples," adding the reason, "for great is his love toward us" (117:2).

Psalm 14 paints a picture of God's heart-longing. He desires His creatures to care about Him: "The LORD looks down from heaven on the sons of men to see if there are any . . . who seek God" (14:2). The Nineteenth Psalm finds that the Maker's heavens and skies testify everywhere "day after day" and "night after night." David writes, "There is no speech or language where their voice is not heard. Their voice goes out into all the earth, their words to the ends of the world" (19:1-4). It is that kind of coverage Jesus wants for his gospel by those he considered "the light of the world" (Matt. 5:14).

Optimistically another Messianic Psalm, previewing Christ's coming crucifixion, predicts: "All the ends of the earth will remember and turn to the LORD, and all the families of the nations will bow down before him." The Psalmist foresees, "Posterity will serve him; future generations will be told about the LORD. They will proclaim his righteousness to a people yet unborn" (22:27-31). Since "the earth is the LORD's, and everything in it, the world, and all who live in it" (24:1), how could any worshiper leave the Jerusalem temple or the local synagogue without expecting the Object of his or her praise to let His grace spill over to everyone? After all, "God is the King of all the earth" and "reigns over the nations" (47:7-8). After all, God, "created the north and the south" (89:12), "east and west" (107:3), and "the distant shores" (97:7).

The God of Israel "sees all mankind" and "watches all who live on earth" (33:13-14). He longs to "be exalted among the nations . . . [and] in the earth" (46:10). That this longing will not forever be disappointed is the assurance of Psalm 65: "O you who hear prayer, to you all men will come. . . . O God our Savior, the hope of all the ends of the earth and of the farthest seas" (65:2,5). Is not world evangelization the constant drumbeat of the Psalmist? Listen to the music rising from each Jewish home: "May God be gracious . . . that your ways may be known on earth, your salvation among all nations. . . . May all the peoples praise you. May the nations be glad and sing for joy" (67:1-7).

The invitation to worship is not for but a select few. It rather is, "O kingdoms of the earth, sing praise to the Lord" (68:32). The conquest of the one greater than Solomon "will rule from sea to sea . . . to the ends of the earth . . . all nations will serve him" (72:8,11). The invitation to come praise is not only to the small nation of Israel. It rather reads, "Let all the neighboring lands bring gifts to the One to be feared" (76:11). The RSVP on the invitation includes "a future generation . . . a people not yet created" (102:18).

Of God it is said, "all nations are your inheritance" (82:8). Of the future it is written, "All the nations you have made will come and worship before you, O LORD" (86:9). Of "all the kings of the earth," it is prayed, "May they sing of the ways of the LORD" (138:4-5). Of every size and class of the human race, it is hoped there will be exclusion of no "kings of the earth and all nations . . . princes and all rulers on earth, young men and maidens, old men and children" (148:11).

With a song book like Psalms in Jesus' heart, home, synagogue and temple, it is not inconsistent with his upbringing that following his resurrection his commission is to "all the world" and "all creation" (Mark 16:15). Many a time Christ must have pondered the scope of his hymnody: "Declare his glory among the nations, his marvelous deeds among all peoples" (96:3). While Jesus' body during the Incarnation did not roam great distances to Eastern Europe, Polynesian Islands or distant continents, his mind ever sang of the "families of nations" (96:7) and "the distant shores" (98:3). No few square miles of land between the Jordan River and Mediterranean Sea could satisfy his dreams, since "the earth is the LORD's and everything in it" (24:1).

Profit from the Prophets about World Outreach

Each Sabbath day Jesus would go to the local synagogue. Besides the Psalms, there would be readings from the Law and the Prophets. That means that week after week his ears heard songs regarding Gentiles coming to God and his eyes viewed prophecies of that same missionary thrust. He learned of Jeremiah "appointed as a prophet to the nations" (Jer. 1:5), who predicted "all nations" would "gather in Jerusalem to know the name of the LORD" (3:17; 4:2). He was taught of Jonah the missionary to Ninevites and Daniel doing foreign work in Babylon.

Let the roll call of Prophets begin. Hosea knew that "in the place where it was said to them, 'you are not my people,' they will be called, 'sons of the living God.'" (1:10). He heard Jehovah promise, "I will show my love to the one I called 'Not my loved one.' I will say to those called, 'Not my people,' 'You are my people'; and they will say, 'You are my God'" (2:23). Joel spoke of God pouring out his Spirit on all people (2:28). Obadiah prophesied of the day of the Lord "for all nations" in judgment, while Jonah wrote of being "concerned about" a great foreign city (4:11). Micah said,

15

"Many nations will come" (4:2ff) and that God's "greatness will reach the ends of the earth. And he will be their peace" (5:4-5). Habakkuk foresaw that "the earth will be filled with the knowledge of the glory of the LORD, as the waters cover the sea" (2:14), while Zephaniah caught the vision that "the nations on every shore will worship him, every one in its own land" (2:11). Haggai received the foreglimpse that "the desired of all nations will come" (2:7) and Malachi agreed that God's name would "be great among the nations, from the rising to the setting of the sun" (1:11).

Scanning the prophet Zechariah's work, you learn that "Many nations will be joined with the LORD" (2:11) for He is "the LORD of the whole world" (6:5). He speaks of "many peoples and powerful nations" coming "to seek the LORD Almighty and to entreat him" (8:22). While Zechariah talks more of the Gentiles outside of Zion coming to the temple, rather than Jewish worshipers going from their land to the Gentiles, the whole world learning of the true God is evident. The same prophet foresees the triumphal entry of Christ into Jerusalem, writing, "Your King comes to you, righteous and having salvation, gentle and riding on a donkey. . . . He will proclaim peace to the nations. His rule will extend from sea to sea and . . . to the ends of the earth" (9:9-10). He concludes, "The LORD will be king over the whole earth. On that day there will be one LORD and his name the only name" (14:9).

Ezekiel three times asserts, "the nations will know" (36:23; 38:23; 39:7). Daniel tells of God's future kingdom filling "the whole earth" (2:35), as well as enduring "forever" (2:44). He foresees Jesus' ascension, when he is "given authority, glory and sovereign power," with the promised result that "all peoples, nations and men of every language worshiped him" (7:14, cp. 7:27).

The most insightful of all the prophets on the topic of world evangelization is the evangelist of the Old Testament, Isaiah. The Messiah of Matthew, Mark, Luke and John is the same Christ Isaiah describes beforehand. One is struck not only by the passages that relate to the birth of the Messiah and his sacrificial death for mankind, but also by his vision of the world mission to follow. The Messianic reign will succeed and "all nations will stream to it" (2:2), "rally" (11:10) and "hasten" (55:5) to its King.

The borders of God's kingdom will be so extensive that only words like "many peoples" (2:4), "ends of the earth" (24:16; 49:6), or "all mankind" (40:5) describe them. The God of unquenchable love cannot rest until "the whole earth is full of his glory" (6:3). His Son will center a ministry, suggestively, in "Galilee of the Gentiles," where "the people walking in darkness" shall see "a great light" (9:1-2; 42:6). But, the dawn that breaks in Galilee will keep brightening the day until "the earth will be full of the knowledge of the LORD as the waters cover the sea" (11:9).

The book of Isaiah includes hymns admonishing, "Make known among the nations what he has done . . . let this be known to all the world" (12:4-5). There are songs announcing, "The LORD Almighty will prepare a feast of rich food for all peoples. . . . The Sovereign LORD will wipe away the tears from all faces" (25:6,8). The residents of Palestine are not alone the objects of God's grace, for as Isaiah writes, "In his law the islands will put their hope" (42:4,10), as will "the desert and its towns" (42:11). Jews in "the east . . . west . . . north . . . and to the south" (43:5-6) are in on the good news. All people "from the rising of the sun to the place of its setting" (45:6) will feel the warmth of their Maker's invitation, "Turn to me and be saved, all you ends of the earth" (45:22). Let "every knee . . . bow" and "every tongue . . . swear" (45:23). Let "distant nations" hear (49:1), "kings . . . rise up" and "princes . . . bow down" (49:7), for "the Sovereign LORD . . . will beckon to the Gentiles" (49:22).

The latter sections of Isaiah, especially, reveal the missionary reach of God's arms to the last and the least. He writes, "All the ends of the earth will see the salvation of our God"

(52:10). He pens, "Let no foreigner who has bound himself to the LORD say, 'The LORD will surely exclude me from his people'" (56:3). The words from God continue, "My house will be called a house of prayer for all nations" (56:7). The final chapter of Isaiah again makes reference to "all nations and tongues" (66:18). It tells of the proclamation of God's glory "among the nations" (66:19), resulting in the glad result that week after week and month after month "all mankind will come and bow down" before God (66:23).

For many years the Bible has been called a best seller. The one thing I know is that God's Book in its Old and New Testament sections is the best seller of the concept of foreign missions. What has been anticipated in the Sacred Scriptures of Old Covenant days comes into even clearer focus in the church's New Testament Writings. In those texts God's purposing to reach His world with redemption's message blazes forth on every page.

PART ONE

The Gospels as Missionary *Sermons*

CHAPTER 1

The Story God Wanted His World to Hear

What the Old Testament anticipated, the New Testament proclaims loud and clear. God's love for the whole world has led to the sending of His Son into history to redeem the lost through his sinless life, atoning death and victorious resurrection. This story that God wanted His world to hear is the message His church has been commissioned to tell.

The story is called "the gospel," because it is good news indeed. The penmen (Matthew, Mark, Luke and John) are termed the evangelists, for they communicate that glad tidings. What the Ancient Prophets foretold about the suffering Redeemer in word and typology, the Apostolic church preached as accomplished fact. The testimony of a Savior is "a song to be sung to the nations"[1] no longer in *pianissimo*, but in triple *forte*! I am reminded of a member of the Gideon organization, who made a play on the words "hymn book" and affirmed that his whole Bible was in fact a "Him Book," for it was all about Him (Jesus).

Frederick W. Robertson believed "Scripture is full of Christ. From Genesis to Revelation everything breathes of Him, not every letter of every sentence, but the spirit of every chapter." What is true to some degree of all portions of

---

[1]"We've a Story to Tell to the Nations" by Colin Sterne in *Favorite Hymns*, Number Two (Cincinnati: Standard, 1942), p. 57.

Sacred Scripture is most certainly the case of the *genre* of the Bible we call the Gospels.

The Oral Gospel

The story of Jesus crucified and risen was told long before it was written. The good news — the sensational news — "The greatest story ever told" — cried out to be told immediately to every ear that would listen. "Faith comes from hearing the message," according to Romans 10:17. "In the beginning was the sermon," observes Carl H. Morgan.[2] Books often claim that the church produced the Gospels, not the Gospels that created the church. Do not be mislead by a half-truth. It is true that there were many followers of Christ before the first Gospel account was put in writing. However, that gospel message had to be heard before there could be any Christians.

Which came first, the chicken or the egg? Which came first, the written Gospels or believers in the gospel? It stands to reason that when Mary Magdalene saw her crucified Savior alive on resurrection morning, her first response was not to write a book for later generations to read. Rather, as you would expect, "Mary Magdalene went to the disciples with the news: 'I have seen the Lord!' And she told them that he had said these things to her" (John 20:18).

The "lip to ear" rehearsing of the happy news naturally preceded the "pen to eye" accounts that were to follow. Time was of the essence. People needed to hear the Church's story: "You are important to God. Sin's separation can be overcome. Jesus' cross and resurrection have accomplished your atonement, if you will but receive it." The wondrous story, of what God had established for you through His Son, is not too

---

[2]Carl H. Morgan, *The Layman's Introduction to the New Testament* (Valley Forge: The Judson Press, 1968), p. 19.

good to be true. It is too true and good not to be told immediately.

That the glad tidings was meant first to be spoken before it was written was not only logical; it was in many cases necessary. Not every human was literate, but very few of all mankind had no ears to hear. In Christ's day, not everyone could read and write. Until as recently as the past three centuries, few have had that ability. Walter J. Ong recently wrote in a scholarly journal, "Although the Bible lies at the heart of Christianity, over the centuries by far most Christians have been illiterate."[3]

The Written Gospels

When the gospel story came to be written, it did not change its character from a sermon to a biography. The tellers of that glad story did not alter their minds and hearts from being passionate tellers of Christ's passion to becoming unmoved objective historians. They were neither uninvolved emotionally with the Jesus of whom they wrote, nor unconcerned about their reader's acceptance or rejection of their message. What the oral proclaimers felt for their listening hearers, the writing evangelists were feeling for their hoped for readers. Does it surprise you to learn that the material on Jesus' thirty-three and a half years of life from all four Evangelists gives information for approximately thirty some days? It would be far different, if the Gospels were intended to be a "Life of Jesus" primarily. However, it makes sense, when the writer's purpose is to preach the grand story of Jesus' passion for the lost, presenting just enough data from his life that the reader can know who it was that died for him or her.

---

[3]"Text As Interpretation: Mark and After" in *Semia 39* (Decatur, GA: Scholars Press, 1987), p. 22.

Reading between the Lines

As we consider each Gospel individually, we will at once see that there is only one gospel, although there are in our New Testament four Gospels. That is, while there is but one God, one faith, one story, there are different accounts of that saving message. Each single Gospel is a variant on the single story of redemption. Each evangelist looks through a different pair of eyes, but he looks at the same God-man named Jesus. At an old pump organ, I can play one hymn with certain organ-stops pulled out and, then, run through the same song again with other stops out. Anyone listening can tell each time that it is the same melody, only the tone sounds are very different. Matthew's account has a unique sound and is not the same as John's. Luke's and Mark's writings also have a distinctive quality to them. But, readers over the centuries notice, without question, that the one of whom they each write is the same Lord who has transformed them all.

Jesus of Nazareth is not the one who writes any of these evangelistic testimonies, but he is the one about whom all of them speak with fervor. It is correct to recognize each work as evangelistic in intention, apologetic in nature and even propagandistic in the better sense of that word, meaning spreading abroad what the writer felt compelled to share.

When Frederick C. Grant wrote of *The Gospels: Their Origin and Their Growth*, he agreed: "These writers were the protagonists, the propagandists, the missionaries, the teachers, the preachers and devoted advocates of a new religious faith."[4] The equally respected C.F.D. Moule, describing one of the Gospels, stated, "This is at once less and much more than a mere narrative: it is a declaration about the significance of a few events. . . . It springs straight from Christian witness: it is the elaboration of a herald's announcement."[5]

---

[4]Frederick C. Grant, *The Gospels: Their Origin and Their Growth* (New York: Octagon Books, 1983), p. 3.

[5]C.F.D. Moule, *The Birth of the New Testament* (New York: Harper and Row, Publishers, 1962), p. 6.

Floyd V. Filson worded it, "The story was told, and the Gospels were finally written by men of faith, to call others to faith and build Christians up in the faith they had accepted."[6] William Owen Carter recognized the Gospels as "missionary handbooks," adding, "We must not forget that their primary purpose and first use was as evangelistic tracts for use of the missionary cause."[7]

We are justified in calling the four Gospels missionary sermons, not because they were written in the first case for the unbeliever to read, but because they were recorded for assisting the Christians in their ministry of outreach to the lost. What John wrote, as the purpose statement for his Gospel account, could be recognized as the same intention of the Synoptic writers: "These (signs of Jesus) are written that you may believe that Jesus is the Christ, the Son of God, and that by believing you may have life in his name" (John 20:31). Matthew, Mark, Luke and John were people who believed in Christ, putting in their "memoirs," concerning Jesus' message and meaning, the material they believed would help other believers in their ministry of carrying out the Risen Christ's great commission.

Each Gospel presents Christ as a friend of sinners. Each evangelist is hoping for all in his audience to become aware: "This is what Jesus has done for you and this is what you ought to do for him." Each portion of a Gospel, as well as the individual Gospel as a whole, is disclosing God as acting in Christ for the reader's redemption. I like the way Ralph P. Martin put it: "The Gospels are written . . . by men of faith in order to convert and confirm their readers by introducing them to the treasure they themselves have found."[8]

---

[6]Floyd V. Filson, *Opening the New Testament* (Nashville: The Westminster Press, 1952), p. 28.

[7]William Owen Carter, *Why They Wrote the New Testament* (Nashville: Convention Press, 1946), p. 58.

[8]Ralph P. Martin, *New Testament Foundations: A Guide for Christian Students: Volume 1* (Grand Rapids: William B. Eerdmans Publishing Co., 1975), p. 48.

Reading between the Lines

Those who love "to tell the old, old story of Jesus and his love,"[9] eventually come to realize that they will not be around forever to tell it. What they put in writing would outlive them. As the witnesses of Apostolic times would be taken by death from this globe in due season, only that portion of their witness recorded in writing would keep talking for them once they were gone. If Moses being dead, yet speaks through his writings, according to Hebrews 11:4, then the testimonies heard from firsthand witnesses in Apostolic days can continue their converting power when preserved in writing. Thomas Brooks saw clearly that "Books may preach when the author *cannot*, when the author *may* not, when the author *dares* not, yea, and which is more, when the author *is* not."

We notice that when worshipers assemble and hear a reading from the Gospels in a church service, they hear more than some preacher's human voice in their ear; they mentally travel across the centuries and experience an inward hearing of the voice of their Savior speaking to their heart. The Gospels, in written form, were still intended to be heard by the masses, rather than to be read from private copies in their homes. The warm human voice of a reader became the voice of Christ to each listening ear. The presence of Jesus was experienced as his words of long ago transformed the past into the present.

The Needed Gospelers

One gospel. Four Gospels. Many Gospelers. That is to say, the one story that God wanted His world to hear has been preserved in the Bible's Four Gospels, so that the Christians of every generation will have needed tools to accomplish the successful evangelizing of their own day and time. What

---

[9]As Catherine Hankey's gospel hymn concludes.

Matthew, Mark, Luke and John wrote to enable the winning
of converts, has served those converts in preparing them to
reproduce themselves. Each author had come to the conclusion that he could not imagine himself trying to live without
Christ and could not think of others trying to live without
him. It had been the Gospel penmen's hope that, like a chain
reaction, each Gospel reader would become a Gospel teller.
The good news is good news for all and so the gospel
demands Gospelers.

S. Vernon McCasland correctly caught the impression that
every person in every corner of the earth was to be included
in the outreach of God. He noted:

> The genius of Christianity is its universality and its sole
> concern is the redemption of individual men. The central
> theme in the teaching of Jesus is the love of God for every
> human being. Christianity repudiated the nationalism from
> which Judaism has never been able to escape; from the
> beginning it has also been an interracial gospel; and it has
> regarded the whole world as its field.[10]

The New Testament's one idea is that the lost world has a
redeeming Savior and his name is Jesus. He is not simply a
figure who lived in the past, long ago. He is a present
Redeemer. At this very hour he stands ready to receive the
repentant sinner, both giving present help and future hope.
Luther knew this as he penned in his *Preface to the New
Testament* of 1522, "No poor fellow chained in sin, dead, and
bound for hell can ever hear anything more comforting and
encouraging than this precious and lovely message about
Christ."

Do you see yourself as a fisherman seeking to catch men
(Matt. 13:47-48) or as a servant inviting guests into God's
house (Luke 14:21-24)? Have you visualized your work as that

---

[10]S. Vernon McCasland, "New Testament Times" in *The Interpreter's Bible Volume
VII*, p. 99.

of a builder, adding stone upon stone to the expanding temple of God (1 Cor. 3:9-11) or as a branch bearing fruit after its kind (John 15:5,8)? Each figure Bible writers have used to define the believer, makes plain that missionary activity is the purpose of the church. "The Spirit of Christ," wrote Henry Martyn, "is the spirit of missions, and the nearer we get to him the more intensely missionary we must become."

It is no accident that each of the four Gospel accounts climax with a great commission word for those hearing the incredible story of God's love to pass it on. The Gospel record best known in Syria called on the reader to "make disciples of all nations" (Matt. 28:19). That identified with Rome called for preaching "to all creation" (Mark 16:15). The word for Greek ears was that "forgiveness of sins" was to be the story heard in "all nations, beginning at Jerusalem" (Luke 24:47). The Roman province of Asia knew they, like Peter, were to "feed" and "care" for the sheep of God (John 21:15-17). Word it any way you please and you arrive at R.H. Glover's definition: "Christian missions is the proclamation of the Gospel to the unconverted everywhere according to the command of Christ."

Let us look now, one by one, at the individual Gospel stories in the order they appear in your New Testament.

CHAPTER 2

The Gospel According to Matthew
God's Reach for the Jewish Mind

The church at Antioch of Syria, where Paul began his several missionary journeys, is the place where some tradition suggests Matthew may have produced his finished Gospel. At least Ignatius of Antioch, in the early years of the second century, attributed the work to him. It was the best known Gospel in Syria in early centuries. Before completing our present Gospel in Antioch, and while still ministering in Palestine, Matthew had produced a brief Aramaic account of Jesus' teaching[1] which he appears to have wedded to Mark's Gospel's account of Christ's deeds (600 of Mark's 661 verses are again found in Matthew). This completed work is often dated around A. D. 80, but some would place it up to three decades earlier.

Matthew, in the present arrangement of New Testament books, appears first and has been listed first since the second century, but it may not be the first Gospel to have been written any more than Paul's letters, following the four Gospels, came after them in time. Such is not the case. The Gospels are placed first, because who would care to read correspondence between Christians before they had an interest in Christ. Matthew gained the primary position because in early days it was the most often quoted and the most widely known

[1]Eusebius tells of Papias reporting such oracles (Logia).

of the four. But, also, it makes the ideal story of Jesus to be sandwiched between the Jewish Scriptures and the other Christian writings.

First for the Jew[2]

Written with the Jew in mind, the Gospel keeps pointing to the fulfillment of the ancient prophecies. The first sentence Matthew pens calls Jesus the "Christ," or "Messiah," and ties him by lineage to "David" and to "Abraham" (1:1). I believe that, as a memory aid, our author divides the genealogical list into three sections of "fourteen generations" (1:17), because the name David has the numerical value of fourteen. The Hebrew alphabet letters could be used as numbers. The D (or Daleth) and the V (or Waw), being the fourth and sixth letters of the Hebrew alphabet, would be added together D+V+D, or 4+6+4, to equal fourteen. King David's seed — the Messiah — was to reign over the whole earth. Therefore that fact is prefigured by the "Magi from the east" coming to Jerusalem "to worship" this heir of David's throne (2:1-2).

The hopes and dreams given to Abraham, Isaac, Jacob and the Israelites are shown to come to pass in this person around whose birth we date all history. The phrase, "Then what was said through the prophet . . . was fulfilled" (2:17) echoes throughout the book, each time having the result of the Jewish reader perceiving that the long-ago promises of God were coming to pass as the Evangelist said. Christian missionaries found Matthew's listing of Old Testament proofs of Jesus' Messiahship the more usable everywhere since the quotations from the Hebrew Bible were from the Septuagint, a Greek translation readable to most of the literate who read Greek.

---

[2]Romans 1:16; 3:29; 15:8-9

Concern for the citizens of the synagogues is further seen in references to "the lost sheep of Israel" (15:24; 16:6), but even more in the parallels drawn also with Moses. Was the infant Moses rescued from a wicked king (Pharaoh)? So was the baby Jesus delivered from the tyrant Herod. Was Moses led from Egypt to the Land of Promise? So was the child Jesus returned from his sojourn with Joseph and Mary in Egypt to Galilee. Did Moses at Mount Sinai bring God's law to the people of Israel? Then follow Jesus to a mountain in Galilee to teach a higher law in his sermon on the mount. Did Moses give Israel the Pentateuch (Five Books of the Law)? Then Matthew will include in his story of Jesus, the new deliverer, five of his teachings (Matt. 5-7; 10; 13; 18-19; 24-25).

From the genealogical list in Chapter 1 to the confession of faith in Jesus as the Messiah in Chapter 16, the reader is led to see that Jesus is the awaited Messiah. The remainder of the book wants the ones who confess Jesus as Christ to know what kind of Messiah he is. He will not be the Military Messiah of Pharisean expectations who they wanted to come and rid the Jewish nation of Roman domination. Rather he was intended by God to be the suffering Messiah who would deliver the people from their sins.

Notice with care that, after Jesus' disciples have been under his teaching and have observed his miraculous powers for two and a half years, they have drawn the only conclusion possible: He is "the Christ, the Son of the living God" (16:16). Jesus concurs with their decision and asserts that the church will be built on that solid-rock foundation. With that fact established, Christ is ready to give his last year of ministry a new direction. Matthew writes, "From that time on Jesus began to explain to his disciples that he must go to Jerusalem and suffer many things . . . be killed and on the third day be raised to life" (16:21). The remaining chapters clarify the type of Messiah he will be. The followers are not to expect a throne for their king in Jerusalem, but a cross. The long-awaited kingdom of heaven, that had been heralded by John the Baptist, Jesus and his disciples, would be spiritual in nature with the crucified and risen Savior reigning from the heavenly Jerusalem, rather than from the earthly Jerusalem which had rejected her king.

Then for the Gentile

The Messiah's reign was to be over all the world. From Christ's genealogy, where four non-Israelite women are included (1:3,5,6), to the final marching orders to baptize "all nations" (28:19), this inclusive idea reigns. The citizenry was to be "the salt of the earth" and "the light of the world" (5:13-14), not just the salt and light of the Mideast. That light was to be seen by men and attract them to the Father in heaven. That salt was to penetrate and affect all persons with whom it came in contact. They were to pray to God, "Your will be done on earth," not alone in Palestine. The Master Teacher instructed his followers to anticipate "that many will come from the east and the west, and will take their places at the feast with Abraham, Isaac and Jacob in the kingdom of heaven" (8:11). Jesus expected that the story of his anointing at Bethany would be more than an incident known across town. It would be one of the treasured memories of people "wherever this gospel is preached throughout the world" (26:13).

Anyone listening to the Lord as he taught would have caught the scope of his vision. There would be the time before his passion when, in the training of the twelve, it would be appropriate to give a limited commission for a brief time, saying, "Do not go among the Gentiles or enter any town of the Samaritans. Go rather to the lost sheep of Israel" (10:6). But once the word Messiah would begin to bring forth images of the cross, redemption and forgiveness, rather than raging warfare against Jewish oppressors, then time would be ripe for the lasting great commission to "all nations" (28:19). When the subject of the teacher from Nazareth was God's coming kingdom, the target for spiritual conquest is given: "The field is the world" (13:38). When the end of the age is painted in living color, Jesus depicts "all nations of the earth will mourn" (24:30) and be "gathered before him" (25:32). When history ends and eternity begins, angels "will gather the elect from the four winds, from one end of heaven to the other" (24:31). And before history comes to a close, the Lord of history foretells, "This gospel of the kingdom will be preached in the whole world as a testimony to all nations, and then the end will come" (24:14). Such words give explanation to the question of the church's proper use of the time remaining up to the final end of history. Our single task is missions. If the climax of time will find the Son of Man commissioning angels to "gather his elect from the four winds, from one end of the heaven to the other" (24:31), the present days, while time remains, are for Christians, as *evangelists*, to cover the same vast expanse and gather converts into the church.

Because the mission is to go to all corners of the globe, "Go to the street corners and invite to the banquet anyone you can find . . . both good and bad" (22:9-10). "Speak in the daylight . . . proclaim from the roofs" (10:27). The Isaiah prophecy rightly foresaw that "in his name the nations will put their hope" (12:21 cp. 18). There is significance in the fact that the Lord's earthly ministry, although aimed at his own nationality during those incarnate days, centered in "Galilee of the Gentiles" (4:15).

After the crucifixion and resurrection the false idea of an earthly kingdom, held by Jesus' contemporaries, would fade and the true nature of the gospel would be ready for world consumption. Thus the great or final commission is given to cover the earth with the story. According to Matthew 28:18-20, evangelizing the nations is the way Christ's regal rule is to be extended on this planet.

"Go and make disciples" are the words of the commission

at the end of this Gospel, as "Go to the street corners and invite" are the words of an earlier parable. Intersections, city centers or crossroads conjure up the scenes of the crowds of humankind that make up the Gentile masses. If the Divine instruction to the first Adam was, "Be fruitful and increase in number; fill the earth" (Gen. 1:28), the bride of the second Adam (the church) hears similar orders from the Lord of heaven in the last paragraph of Matthew's Gospel. The last word of the account is not Christ's resurrection, but his followers' mission. The encouraging sound of Christ's final commission is that he who commands is he who does enable: "I am with you always, to the very end of the age" (28:20).

John R.W. Stott is probably correct in his assessment: "We engage in evangelism today not because we want to or because we choose to or because we like to, but because we have been told to."[3] Christ's authority is the launching pad for the story God wants to circle the earth. The last words from Jesus' lips constitute the great commission and not simply a good suggestion.

Matthew wants the reader, or hearer, of his Gospel to put himself in the shoes of the eleven disciples, who heard these words spoken on a mountain in Galilee, and get busy at the challenging task of discipling, baptizing and teaching all ethnic groups of earth. He hopes for the churches to measure all their busy, multiple activities by the criterion of the King of king's final command.

May the congregation where you worship in these modern times become incurably missionary minded, as Matthew desired the congregations in Apostolic days to be. An unmissionary church cannot claim to be a Christian church, in that the term implies submission to Christ. The Devil is on his mission of destruction everywhere on earth. Let the messen-

---

[3]John R.W. Stott, "The Great Commission" in Carl F. H. Henry and W. Stanley Mooneyham, Editors, *One Race, One Gospel, One Task Volume I* (Minneapolis: World Wide Publications, 1967), p. 37.

gers of Christ's deliverance leave no spot on the globe untouched. The marching orders are clear. Let our marching feet hasten in obedience.

CHAPTER 3

The Gospel According to Mark
God's Reach for the Roman Mind

It was said, "All roads lead to Rome." But those persons under Christ's commission to win the world, sought to find the best road to reach the Roman mind, or the Jewish mind, or the mindset of the peoples they desired to evangelize. Matthew took the high road of fulfilled prophecy, as one route his blood-related Jewish friends might walk in coming to their Messiah. In Mark's short story, penned from Rome and to the Romans, his desire was to map the trail most apt to be followed by Romans to their world's Savior. Their ideal was power and action, so Mark will hold before their eyes the more than adequate power and the seemingly endless energy of Jesus in his ministry of miracles. Mark's message was destined to transform persons, who held in highest esteem the love of power, and turn them into people captured by the power of love.

That Mark is targeting Romans, and other readers many miles from Palestine, is noticed in several places in his written document. Aramaic expressions are interpreted for readers, who otherwise would not know their meaning (5:41; 7:34; 15:34). Jewish customs are explained, lest the non-Jew miss the teaching (7:3-4,11; 14:12; 15:42). Jewish names are given with their meaning made clear (3:17; 15:22). And today's linguists, alert to "Latinisms," point out that Mark spells out the Latin words in Greek characters to more adequately catch the attention of the residents of Rome.

The Power of Christ's Message

This Gospel is rightly labeled preaching. The opening chapter begins with the preaching of John the Baptist (1:2-8) and the closing chapter concludes with "the Eleven" (16:14) being instructed to "preach . . . to all" (16:15), which Mark reports "the disciples" did "everywhere" (16:20). Between these beginning and end statements about the proclaiming done by the prophet in the desert to the heralding accomplished by the apostles, Mark tells of Jesus preaching.

Once the Baptist's voice is silenced by imprisonment under Herod at Machaerus, Jesus picks up the torch, going "into Galilee proclaiming the good news of God" (1:14). Almost immediately, he begins to gather men he will train to preach, promising, "I will make you fishers of men" (1:18). His model teaching, plus his priorities in ministry, will tutor those to become his witnesses.

When the people put the miracles in the first place of importance, Jesus chooses the power of preaching as of the highest order. He advises, "Let us go somewhere else — to the nearby villages — so I can preach there also. That is why I have come" (1:38). Picking twelve and "designating them apostles," he had them under his tutelage "that he might send them out to preach" (3:14).

With preaching so prominent in this book before us, at first one is surprised to find so few of Christ's sermons or parables in this Gospel, when Matthew's contained so many. Then you remember Mark is selecting from his rich resources of memories that which will have special appeal to Romans. These, who might not have time for birth-stories (as did Matthew and Luke) and little time for contemplating profound teaching (as important as that is), will have time and interest in the fast-paced and exciting adventures of the vigorous hero who wins verbal battles with all his opponents and courageously moves from one conflict to another.

While Mark does not give many sermons of length by the

Master, he always describes the powerful effect Jesus' words had on others every time he spoke. If the Lord utters the single word, "Ephphatha!," deaf ears hear and mute lips speak (7:34). If this man but orders, "Talitha koum!" (5:41), those words, at once, transform a dead girl into a vibrant young lady. The reader is to imply that such life-changing results happen whenever and wherever that now-resurrected Christ's story is told.

Papias is probably correct in recognizing that the written Gospel by Mark is the record of the oral proclamation of the Apostle Peter. The tradition is, that when the voice of the big fisherman was silenced by his being crucified upside down under Nero in Rome, A. D. 64, the church knew it had lost a great witness of Christ's resurrection. Since Mark, who had earlier been serving under the great apostle Paul and most recently under Simon Peter in Rome (2 Peter 5:13), knew the apostolic testimony, the brethren looked to him to preserve in writing the eyewitness testimony of Peter that he had heard orally so many times. A comparison of the general outline of Mark's Gospel with the preaching of Peter preserved in Acts 2:22-36 and 10:36-43 shows Simon's finger-prints all over this Gospel's story of Jesus' powerful life and cross-centered passion.

The heading of the Gospel, "The beginning of the gospel about Jesus Christ, the Son of God" (1:1), should be suffi-cient to inform the reader that the rest of the document would not be the simple relating of historical facts of little consequence. This is, rather, to be seen as the preaching of the gospel of Christ. His heroic service to people in need and his courageous willingness to die for others is hoped to rivet the reader's attention on that person called "Son of God." This kind of story demands a response. No Roman, mentally taken to the foot of Christ's cross, should hesitate to join with the proud and mighty Roman centurion in the admission, "Surely this man was the Son of God" (15:39).

No modern day evangelist, retelling the same old Christ-exalting, cross-relating gospel, would think of concluding without an invitation to accept such a Savior. This Gospel, like the others, will describe Jesus' passion in great detail. All apostolic preaching hurried to the part of their message that would tell of Jesus' death for our transgressions. Then all that would be left to tell would be the sinners need to believe and be baptized (16:16). A written Gospel is but the written form of apostolic witness.

The Power of Christ's Miracles

The story of God's redeeming love preached by the apostles, is told in the non-verbal communication of Christ's miracles. The power of Roman armies struck fear into all their enemies. The awesome authority of the enthroned Emperors caused trembling in the hearts of any who would not submit to their whims. Now, in Jesus of Nazareth, a totally different kind of power comes onto the stage of world history. It is the combination of power and love. It is evident in every wonder Christ performs.

After pagan troops march through a country, the remaining scenes of destruction are everywhere. Homes are destroyed, women are raped, children cry with a fright not soon to be erased from their minds. "War is hell!" becomes more than a cliché. Poverty, sadness and hopelessness mark the trail. But, in Mark's gospel we see a totally different scene. Blessings abound wherever Jesus and his disciples come. Be it Galilee (1:39), Judea, Idumea, Perea or Phoenicia (3:8), the benefits of the Lord abound. Be it some area in Decapolis (5:1; 7:31) or the region of Dalmanutha (8:10), the tears get wiped away. World power takes lives. Divine power transforms lives.

Mark does not list hundreds of examples of one disease mastered by the Master. He rather tells of an instance of blindness overcome, of a leper finding cleansing or a demon-possessed person freed. By healing a skin disorder here and a blood disorder there, the populace can see that, whatever the difficulty, Jesus can conquer it. A raging storm calmed or a hungry multitude fed shows no difficulty beyond the conquering power of this unique carpenter from Nazareth.

The Christians, who read each healing account preserved by Mark, had a paradigm they could use in telling their hearers of the Savior. Is the populace spiritually blind, morally crippled or fatally diagnosed to have the leprosy of sin? There is no need to despair. Jesus teaches God has sufficient love to want to rescue the afflicted and more than adequate power to solve the difficulty.

Almost a third of Mark's Gospel is composed of healing stories, where a human was in a desperate, incurable situation. There was no inkling of hope. Then Jesus came and the sad story turned out to have the wonderful ending of total and immediate healing. The reader is encouraged to believe that what Jesus did in the short years of his ministry yesterday, he still can do for any person who turns to him today.

When the Gospel near its conclusion quotes Jesus saying baptized believers would be "saved" (16:16), it uses the Greek word meaning "made whole." Each healing story related a person of plight being made whole. The individual was, at the touch of Christ, more than better. He was healed — made whole — saved. The key word of the book is "immediately" (5:42) or "straightway" (KJV). "Instantaneous" and "perfect" are adjectives correctly defining miracles. No blind and dumb man is left by Jesus able to see, but not able to speak. The Lord does no halfway job. A demon-possessed lame man will not be enabled to walk but remain under an evil spirit's power.

Christ, the King of Matthew's Gospel emphasis, is Jesus, the Savior of Mark's account. Both Gospel records make the confession of faith at Caesarea Philippi the turning point (Matt. 16:16; Mark 8:29). The earlier portion of Matthew was to convince the reader that Jesus was the Messiah, while the rest of the story was to clarify the type of Christ he would be.

41

The first half of Mark brings us to the same conclusion of who Jesus is (1:14-8:30) and the final portion (8:31-16:20) to the same verdict that this Christ is the suffering servant that the prophets foretold would be "pierced for our transgressions" and "crushed for our iniquities" (Isa. 53:5). Mark 10:45 becomes a key verse for the Gospel's outline. It reads, "The Son of Man did not come to be served, but to serve, and to give his life a ransom for many." Our powerful Monarch was a servant (the first half of Mark) and a savior (the second portion). The symbol of the ox, often used for this Gospel, is a fitting symbol in that an ox can be harnessed to a plow to pull a load or sacrificed on an altar to be a sacrifice for sin.

The greatest miracle of all was the removal of the sin that separated man from God by Jesus' self-sacrifice on the cross. Has there ever been such love manifest? Has there ever been such drawing power revealed?

The Power of Christ's Mission

It is time to tackle a problem. I earlier wrote that the Gospel before us begins with the preaching of the Baptist (1:1-8), continues with the preaching of Jesus (1:9-16:8), and ends with the preaching of the church (16:9-20). But, does it? While the other Synoptic Gospels conclude with the giving of the great commission (Matt. 28:18-20; Luke 24:45-49), does Mark? The New International Version includes the words of Mark 16:9-20, yet with the disclaimer, "The most reliable manuscripts and other ancient witnesses do not have Mark 16:9-20." Some other translations either omit the passage, relegate it to the bottom of the page or place it within brackets in small type or italics.

To whatever conclusion your personal study leads you, realize no doctrine or practice in these last twelve verses of the text is foreign to the teaching found in the rest of the New Testament. Let us nail down a few facts.

What NIV refers to as "the most reliable early manu-scripts" are Codex Sinaticus (ℵ) and Codex Vaticanus (B). These excellent uncial manuscripts, while ending at Mark 16:8, do leave space for the missing verses, as if conscious that they exist. Weigh the absence of the final twelve verses in these two fourth century Bibles with the fact that other uncials — Codex Alexandrinus (A), Codex Ephraemi (C) and Codex Bezae (D) — do have the verses, as do all the many cursive manuscripts. Keep in mind that, as important as the Sinaticus and Vaticanus are, the manuscripts we do have contain the verses 300 to 1. Add also to your thinking the further fact that there are translations into other languages (Old Latin, Syrian, Coptic) that do contain the questioned verses. These were made from now lost Greek manuscripts that precede in time the ℵ and B referred to. Before you are overwhelmed by the scholarly world's honest doubts, do not forget segments of the missing verses were quoted and known by Tatian[1] (150 A.D.), in his *Diatessaron*, by Iranaeus[2] (177 A.D.), Justin Martyr[3] (160 A.D.) and the Shepherd of Hermas[4] (150 A.D.). It is beyond our present purpose to wrestle with the main points of this debate, but an interested reader is encouraged to investigate the scholarly work of William Farmer entitled *The Last Twelve Verses of Mark*.

It is enough for us to see that post-resurrection appear-ances of Jesus, with their commissioning of believers to evan-gelize, is anticipated in the earlier parts of Mark's Gospel. Mark 8:31, 9:31 and 10:34 make clear that Jesus is to be killed, but "after three days rise again." In 14:28, the Lord predicts, "After I have risen, I will go ahead of you into Galilee" and in 16:28 angels at the empty tomb state, "He is going ahead of you into Galilee. There you will see him, just

---

[1]Mark 16:9-20
[2]Mark 16:19
[3]Mark 16:19-20
[4]Mark 16:16

as he told you."

The absence of the verses in dispute from Sinaticus and Vaticanus may be better explained by the supposition that the earlier scroll from which they copied had been torn accidentally from the original. "That they said nothing to anyone, because they were afraid" (16:8), does not seem to be an adequate conclusion for a testimony from Peter, Mark or any gospel herald.

The "go" and "preach," addressed to the apostles then and the believing community now (16:15), and the "believe" and "be baptized," asked of the convert of that day and this (16:15-16), constitute what is labeled the great commission. It might well be titled the great privilege. For a believer to share the news is an honor. For the first-time hearer to trust in Jesus and submit to the Lord's command of baptism is a joy.

The commentator's often referred to "Messianic secret in Mark" has moved from "don't tell anyone yet" to "tell everyone now!" The time to be silent was prior to Jesus' death. In those years Jesus' understanding of himself as the suffering-servant Messiah, would be warped by the strong popular concept of a militant Christ. This false concept would have drawn the mob to Jesus' side. The multitudes would have presented themselves to him as valiant soldiers against Rome rather than penitent sinners before God. By Mark 16 the time to speak had now come. In the crucifixion, followed by resurrection and shortly to be ascension and coronation, the stumbling block had been removed. Christ's displays of power at the beginning of his ministry could lead to the correct conclusion that Jesus was the Messiah. But, at the same time, that manifestation of power could also have led to the incorrect assumption that God was ready to use his power to destroy Romans rather than redeem them. Now that Jesus has died, not as a martyr to some undefined cause but as the one God sent to show His love to all, the story is ready for its telling.

The message is that whosoever will may come and that

whosoever has come ought now to go in order that others may know the good news. The rejection of the story leaves the hearer the option, "whoever does not believe will be condemned" (16:16). The ultimate destiny is heaven or hell. Modern sentimentalists to the contrary, the damnation option, believed and taught by Jesus, was a large part of the drive behind his mission outreach. The churches, that to this day believe in a possible separation from God termed hell, are sparked to evangelize. Those that have deleted such a consequence from their thinking, flag in zeal to tell of a Savior from sin. They spend their efforts only at social change for man while upon earth. Mark, in reaching for the Roman mind, holds before his readers the eternal consequences. He believes that knowing the end of the roads to be taken will help in starting down the right road.

CHAPTER 4

The Gospel According to Luke
God's Reach for the Greek Mind

Sixty-six books penned by around forty authors make up the Christian's Bible. Sixty-four of them were written by Jews. The two exceptions — Luke and Acts — were written by the one Paul called, "Our dear friend Luke, the doctor" (Col. 4:14).

Harold R. Cook in *An Introduction to the Study of Christian Missions* makes this observation:

> When it comes to Christianity we have a strange phenomenon. It began among the Jews, but most of the Jews have never accepted it. It began in the Orient, but its strongest centers today are in the West. Its Scriptures are very little read in the original languages, but they are read around the world in more than a thousand tongues. [1]

Luke's confession of faith, that we call the Gospel according to Luke, has been a contributing factor to the conversion of many non-Jews. Not being from the covenant people, the evangelist thrills to know that the gospel has reached out even to him. His account will feature what Jesus has done for outsiders. The Gospel may have been written in Corinth. Dates given by students of the Bible range from A.D. 60 to

---

[1] Harold R. Cook, *An Introduction to the Study of Christian Missions* (Chicago: Moody Press, 1954), p. 22.

80. Likely what Luke began to write during Paul's imprisonment in Caesarea was finalized as we now have it at the later date and place. His apparent use of the Gospel of Mark suggests this.

He addresses his Gospel, as he will his second volume called Acts, to some public official that he calls "most excellent Theophilus" (1:3). Luke is interested that this man, and all others who will read Christ's story dedicated to this man of high authority, will "know the certainty" (1:4) that undergirds the Christian faith. The author's desire is that his careful account will be used by the churches in their work of missionary evangelism. He has been with Paul as this missionary of all missionaries has, by God's special call, reached for the Gentiles across the Roman Empire. Luke's longing is for his writings to be literary missionaries holding out hope in Christ for all mankind.

Sons of Adam Have Hope

Where Matthew, with Jews in mind, traces Christ's genealogy back to Abraham; Luke, with Gentiles in his thoughts, reaches even farther back in Jesus' bloodline. The evangelist takes the genealogy all the way to "Adam" (3:38), so that Jesus will have universal relevance to every descendant of the first man.

From the beginning of his book, Luke wants Jesus recognized as more than a Jew of consequence for fellow-Jews. He places this ideal man on the stage of world history. At his birth "Caesar Augustus" is Emperor of the Roman world and "Quirinius" is governing in Syria (2:1-2). When Jesus' ministry begins, "Tiberius Caesar" is reigning in the place of Augustus (Octavian); "Pontius Pilate" is governing Judea; and, Herod the Great's sons, "Herod," "Philip," and "Lysanius," have been given the rule of tetrarchs (3:1-2).

At the birth of Jesus, angels let it be known that the "good news of great joy . . . will be for all the people" (2:10). At the presentation in the temple, Simeon praises God for allowing his eyes to see Jesus. He prays, "My eyes have seen your salvation, which you have prepared in the sight of all the people, a light for revelation to the Gentiles and for glory to your people Israel" (2:30-32). The "and" in that last sentence deserves attention. It is not "either — or." Jesus is for "Gentiles and" Israelites. He is for sons of Adam and also sons of Abraham, Isaac and Jacob.

R.H. Strachan, writing on the Gospel of Luke, points out that Luke's "evangelical motive already makes itself apparent in the nativity hymns of his opening chapter. . . . Luke is everywhere conscious that he is not merely writing a narrative but proclaiming the gospel."[2]

The tempter in the wilderness showed to the newly baptized Messiah "all the kingdoms of the world" (4:5), rather than just the borders of the Jewish nation. Satan knew God's Christ was for the whole world, but he tempted him to build his universal kingdom the satanic way instead of the holy way heaven intended. The mission is the world, but the method is not militarism and materialism. It is, instead, ministry and self-sacrifice.

While Jesus ministers in that small spot of real estate we call Palestine, he keeps speaking of God's universal concern for all the sons of Adam. He relates how in Elijah's ministry in Israel, God's blessing was extended to "Zarephath in the region of Sidon" (4:26) and how in Elisha's service as prophet, God chose to cleanse from leprosy "Naaman the Syrian" (4:27). He emphasizes, for every non-Jew's ears to hear, "People will come from east and west and north and south, and will take their places at the feast in the kingdom of God" (13:29). Lest any person feel unwanted and uninvited, the Teacher's words are, "Go out quickly into the

---

[2]R.H. Strachan, "The Gospel on the New Testament" in *The Interpreter's Bible Vol. VII.*

streets and alleys of the town and bring in the poor, the crippled, the blind and the lame. . . . There is still room. . . . Go out to the roads and country lanes and make them come in, so that my house will be full" (14:21-23). Luke leaves no doubt that God cares for all Gentiles (2:32; 3:6; 24:44), for all women (7:11-12; 8:2-3; 10:38-42) and for all outcasts (10:29-37; 15:1-21; 17:11-19; 18:9-14).

Reader, are you a Jew? Then you know the Messiah's gospel is for you. Are you a Gentile? Luke, the Gentile, wants you to have no doubts about God's message being for you as much as for him. All sons of Adam are on God's invitation list. Race, color and bloodline may not matter. But what about our sin condition? Is there a state where hope is gone?

Lost Sinners Have Hope

The key word of the Gospel is "compassion" and the key verse is 19:10: "For the Son of Man came to seek and to save what was lost." Of the twenty-two parables of Jesus preserved for us in this grand Gospel, none are more evangelistic in thrust than the three on lostness found in Chapter Fifteen. The Savior talked about lost sheep (15:3-7), lost coins (15:8-10) and lost sons (15:11-32). Each of the parables define Christian ministry as seeking for the lost — not entertaining the saved. Each story is a call to the believers to both join Christ in the search for the lost and to share in the jubilation at their recovery.

The setting for this trio of parabolic gems is the criticism coming to Christ for his concept of ministry. The Pharisees and the teachers of the law muttered that Jesus spent his time with the wrong kind of people. To be specific, they blurted, "This man welcomes sinners and eats with them" (15:2). Knife and fork evangelism was one of Christ's effective methods of doing missionary work. Luke wants his readers to see their challenge in following Jesus' compassion toward the lost, accepting them, befriending them, dining with them and pointing their way to forgiveness.

The parable of the ninety and nine stresses the value of the lost "one" and the integral place of going "after the lost sheep until he finds it." Heaven's interest in the sinner and the importance of repentance is underscored. The story of the lost coin holds up the value of a sinner to God, being considered well worth the difficult search. The church is viewed as an extremely happy place, where joy abounds in the recovery of one lost person after another. Conversion is its main business.

The story of the Prodigal Son climaxes the trinity of parables about Jesus' great mercy toward sinners. The late famous missionary strategist, Donald A. McGavran, drew this needed lesson for today's missionaries from Jesus' ancient tale: "The goal is not to send powdered milk or kindly messages to the son in the far country. It is to see him walking in through the front door of his father's house."[3] It is so easy for the Lord's church to substitute the means for the ends, social help for religious conversion. Yet, only as we conform our thoughts to the Lord's thinking, will the "dead" be "alive again," or the "lost" be "found" (15:32).

Distant Foreigners Have Hope

Like the other Synoptic Gospels, Luke's picture of Jesus as the ideal man gives his commission to his followers to share the good news of "repentance and forgiveness of sins . . . to all nations" (24:47). Where Mark specifies "all creation" (16:15) and Matthew directs "all nations," Luke agrees, but adds "beginning at Jerusalem" (24:47). That phraseology gets the reader ready for Luke's second volume named Acts,

---

[3]Donald A. McGavran, *Understanding Church Growth* (Grand Rapids: Eerdmans, 1970), p. 5.

which records the gospel's spread from that key Jewish city to the Roman World's capital in Italy.

In his first chapter Luke introduced us to John the Baptist's father Zechariah in Jerusalem. In the central portion of his Gospel Luke shows Christ's determination to turn his face again to Jerusalem, where his passion will be lived out. Now at the end of the story, it is again in the holy city of Jerusalem where Israel's Messiah will die, rise again, appear to his disciples, commission them and ask them to tarry there for the gift of his Spirit which will enable the assigned mission of world evangelization.

To prepare the reader for the commission that can only be called "Great," Luke prefigures Gentile conversion by speaking well of Samaritans or half-breeds. Jesus taught the parable of the Good Samaritan (10:25-37) and praised the grateful former leper (one of the ten, now healed) adding, "and he was a Samaritan" (17:16), a "foreigner" (17:18). It was because of the Jewish nation's ingratitude that Jesus foresaw the fact that God would "give the vineyard to others" (20:16). Having a ministry in Perea, outside of Israel's territory, and appointing seventy-two to precede him, may have hinted at the coming Gentile mission. Sending out the twelve had implied that the twelve tribes of Israel were in God's plans. Since there were approximately seventy or so world nations at that time, the choice of seventy-two may have suggested the message was for all mankind (10:1).

Now, at the closing of the Gospel, we hear our marching orders that "repentance and forgiveness of sins will be preached in his name to all nations, beginning at Jerusalem" (24:47). J.C. Choate comments, "These are not just words, just more words, just anyone's words. They are different, mighty, powerful, and frightening. They are the words of Jesus, spoken to his disciples yesterday and today, involving the whole earth."[4]

Since all people share our plight of sinfulness, all nations, all languages and all persons have the great need that lies behind the great commission. It has never been superseded or canceled. According to legend, the letters in the word NEWS stand for North, East, West and South. According to Christ, the head of the church, they who knew the good news were to take the story in every direction, "beginning from Jerusalem." According to statisticians, there are more people alive in our twentieth century who have never heard the story than there were living on that day in the first century when the commission was given. The problem is that natural births are outpacing births from above. The solution is for Christians to give missions the priority Christ gave in his last command.

⁴J.C. Choate, *Missionary Preparation* (Winona, MS: J.C. Choate Publications), p. 1.

CHAPTER 5

The Gospel According to John
God's Reach for the Post-Apostolic Mind

Every Christian interested in soul-winning has a special interest in the Gospel according to John. Often that Gospel, printed by itself and not attached to the other Bible books, is used as a tract to be given to a prospective convert. Since it is easy to read, profound in insight and convicting in power, it has been found an excellent tool for winning neighbors and friends to Christ. Also, those who teach believers how to master Jesus' technique in one-on-one evangelism, turn to the fourth chapter of John for the ideal model to follow (4:1-42). Each deliberate step the Lord takes in conversation with the woman at the well, lays out a pattern for those with an evangelistic heart to follow for personal success in this highest of endeavors.

The compulsion for a follower of Jesus to reach out for another with whom faith can be shared is evidenced by the Apostle John. The Baptist passes his faith on to disciples, Andrew invites Peter, Philip finds Nathaniel and one by one the few followers become the many. R. Alan Culpepper, writing about John's Gospel as narrative, comments: "Through the reading experience one is introduced to a wide range of interpretations and responses to Jesus . . . the Gospel, because it is narrative, is a textual strategy or means of evoking an intricate series of responses from the reader . . . as we read we are invited . . . to rehearse various responses to

Jesus' call for faith."[1]

John's openly-expressed purpose in writing Christ's story has been fulfilled again and again from his day until this present hour: "Jesus did many other miraculous signs in the presence of his disciples, which are not recorded in this book. But these are written that you may believe that Jesus is the Christ, the Son of God, and that by believing you may have life in his name" (20:30-31).

As we examine this last of the Gospels, we will be quick to see how different in content it is from the Synoptics. The missionary motive is the same, but the incidents in Christ's life that are told are mostly other than those preserved by Matthew, Mark and Luke. John, writing after these earlier works were penned and circulated, wished to supplement, not duplicate, their memoirs. John is the last apostle alive. Being the last official living witness to the crucified and resurrected Jesus, he will testify in writing to some seven special miracles which enlighten Christ's purpose and meaning. As a member of the apostolic band (and the inner circle at that), John will save for posterity what Jesus said to his men in the upper room and what he prayed for his church before leaving for the garden.

This Gospel, written in John's mature years, has been dated all the way from A.D. 80 to 100, depending on whether it is believed to have come from John's hand before or after his experience on the Isle of Patmos (A.D. 96). A fragment of John 18, dating from the second quarter of the second century, indicates how early John's Gospel was in circulation.[2] Irenaeus (A.D. 185) identifies our author, who only

---

[1]Bernhard W. Anderson, Editor *The Books of the Bible II: The Apocrypha and The New Testament* (New York: Charles Scribner's Sons, 1989), pp. 209-210.

[2]This fragment of five verses is tagged by scholars as $\mathfrak{P}^{52}$. It is preserved in the John Rylands Library of Manchester, England.

refers to himself in his Gospel as "the disciple whom Jesus loved" (21:20), as John the Apostle. Keeping in mind that Irenaeus had heard Polycarp preach, and remembering that Polycarp had known John personally, these facts make the testimony of authorship credible. The Christian center of the Roman province of Asia (modern Turkey), being the city of Ephesus, makes that locale the place of writing. To this, ancient tradition regarding John agrees.

The Changing Times

Before the curtain rises on the great drama of the incarnate Christ, there is the prologue (1:1-14), suggesting major themes to be discussed in this Gospel that concern God's Word become flesh. After the curtain drops at the climax of this passion-resurrection portrayal, there will follow an epilogue (21:1-25). This fact makes the final scene of Jesus' appearance to doubting Thomas (20:24-29) the picture to remain indelibly on the viewer's mind.

Thomas being absent from the room on Resurrection Sunday when the living Lord appeared to his disciples, the apostolic report to him seemed unbelievable. He insisted on firsthand experience, rather than apostolic testimony. Thomas said, "Unless I see the nail marks in his hands and put my finger where the nails were, and put my hand into his side, I will not believe" (20:25). Should men of every nation in post-apostolic times make the same demand, there could be no Christians on earth.

John knows this, for the day of eyewitnesses to the gospel facts will soon be gone. He gives the rest of the story, where Jesus appears one week later to the apostolic band, offering the evidence of sight and touch Thomas had demanded. Thomas is completely convinced and his confession flows freely, "My Lord and my God!" (20:28). If other potential believers refuse belief and insist on sight, the future is bleak.

Christ has no intention of making re-entrances into the world day after day and country after country so there will be followers.

Listen carefully to Jesus' final words as the closing curtain falls. They contain a beatitude never to be forgotten: "Because you have seen me, you have believed; blessed are those who have not seen and yet have believed" (20:29). God's blessing will fall on all who trust the story. Such will "have life in his name."

The vital question is, "can belief in a historic fact be had, if there is credible testimony given by those who were eye-witnesses of that event?" By the time John writes, thousands, who had never seen Jesus with their own eyes, were convinced by the oral testimony of the apostles across the world. Now that all of these, who had walked and talked with Jesus, were being silenced by death, will the faith die out? As the church enters post-apostolic times, John shouts that written apostolic testimony has the same power as oral testimony. He writes, "Jesus did many other miraculous signs in the presence of his disciples, which are not recorded in this book. But these are written that you may believe that Jesus is the Christ, the Son of God, and that by believing you may have life in his name" (20:30-31).

The apostles did not pass on rumors or guesses. What they told was what occurred in their "presence" (20:30). What is "written" testimony has been "written that you may believe" (20:31). Jesus is no longer incarnate on the earth. Those, who saw what he did and heard what he said, have also gone to glory. Yet, in these changed times, millions walk by faith and will do so until that day Christ returns and faith becomes sight again.

John's primary purpose has been thought by some to be the turning of unbelievers into believers, but by others it has been the keeping of Christians true to the Christ the Apostles taught in the face of the challenge being brought by incipient Gnosticism. The deceptive appeal of this rising heresy was that firsthand relations with Jesus was preferable to second-hand testimony, even when it came from eyewitnesses. In other words, experience is better than faith — knowing is preferable to believing.

The scholarly argument rages over variant Greek manuscripts at the point of the word "believing." Some have the word as present subjunctive (i.e., continue to believe). Others have "believing" in the aorist subjunctive (i.e., bring to faith). D.A. Carson in his article, "The Purpose of the Fourth Gospel: John 20:31 Reconsidered," concludes that the Gospel author intended his work to be "an evangelistic tool aimed at converting Hellenistic Jews to Jesus Messiah. I would include as well proselytes and God-fearers."[3] Carson's reasoning is based on John's other uses of the Greek ἵνα with a transitive verb connected with his often used subject of life. Comparing a half-dozen cases in the Gospel,[4] he argues, "Not one of them suggests continuing in life or preserving eternal life . . . applied to 20:31, this observation serves as telling evidence that John wrote his Gospel with evangelistic intent."[5] Yet, even while John might have penned originally the present subjunctive, dealing with persistence in faith, rather than the aorist, referring to the dawn of faith; nevertheless the concern for staying with what the apostles taught about Jesus could well have been related to his missionary purpose.

The Unchanging Goal

Thumb through these twenty-one chapters and be impressed with their whole-world concern. In Chapter One Jesus is shown to have come into "the world" that was "made through him" (1:10). John the Baptist introduces him, who as

[3]*Society of Biblical Literature Volume 106, Number 4* (December, 1987), p. 646.
[4]John 3:15-16; 5:40; 6:60; 10:10; 17:2; 20:31.
[5]*SBL Vol. 106, No. 4*, p. 648.

God's Lamb will give himself to take "away the sin of the world" (1:29). The most familiar of all Jesus' expressions is John 3:16, where God's love for "the world" is the attributed cause for God sending "his one and only Son." This God of the Bible "did not send his Son into the world to condemn the world, but to save the world through him" (3:17; 12:47). Heaven's light was not to illume Palestine alone. God's "light has come into the world" (3:19).

The Samaritan woman knows her Savior to be "the Savior of the world" (4:42). She learned from Christ that "salvation is from the Jews" (4:22), but knew that he who was *from* the Jews was *for* the world. Half-Jew that she is, she had learned the whole truth about this man who talked with her at Jacob's well. In 6:33 Christ claims to be the bread from heaven who "comes down from heaven and gives life to the world" (6:33; cp. 6:51). He who is life for the world is also called "The light of the world" (8:12; 9:5; 12:46) that will tell "the world" whatever his Father told him (8:26).

During the limited days of earthly ministry, the Teacher was ever looking to the future when the whole earth could know of him. "I have other sheep that are not of this sheep pen," he foretold (10:16). John commented on what Caiaphas as high priest had said that "Jesus would die for the Jewish nation." He added the words, "And not only for that nation but also for the scattered children of God" (11:51-52).

The Gospel of John sees the crucified Christ "lifted up from the earth" to "draw all men" to himself (12:32). It sees the Holy Spirit's coming to "convict the world" regarding Jesus (16:8), as Jesus had "entered the world" (16:28) and the apostles would bear their testimony "in this world" (16:33). John saves for our eyes to read the high-priestly prayer and its concern for the mission. Jesus intercedes for himself, as he extends his "authority over all people that he might give eternal life" (17:2). He intercedes for his witnesses that he sent "into the world" as he had been sent by the Father "into the world" (17:18). He asks "that the world may believe"

(17:21) — that "world" where Christ had made the Father "known" (17:25-26) and where the Church's unity will "let the world know" of the Father's love for them (17:23).

It is not without significance that the words fastened to the cross reading, "JESUS OF NAZARETH, THE KING OF THE JEWS," was written "in Aramaic, Latin and Greek" (19:20). That message, like this Gospel, was for all to read. Everyone ought to know who Jesus is.

If everything Jesus had done in eternity and time had been written down, "even the whole world would not have room for the books" (21:25). But in God's heavenly home there "are many rooms" (14:2), so let the saved remain busy at their task of reaching out for every lost man. David Livingstone is reported to have said, "God had only one Son, and He was a missionary." We have found that the New Testament has four Gospel accounts, and all of them are missionary in intent. Not all four tell of Jesus' birth, baptism, temptation or parables, but every one details the cross, resurrection and commissioning. In John these saving events of death and resurrection are anticipated as "the hour"[6] when man's redemption is obtained.

---

[6]John 2:4; 4:21,23; 5:25,28; 7:30; 8:20; 12:23,27; 13:1; 17:1

PART TWO

The Acts as
Missionary *Records*

CHAPTER 6

Luke, the Missionary Historian

Luke wanted Theophilus, and all who would read that Gospel dedicated to him, to realize that it told only what "Jesus began to do and teach" (Acts 1:1). The crucified and risen Lord had completed his earthly mission by giving his followers the assignment of preaching "repentance and forgiveness of sins . . . to all nations, beginning at Jerusalem" (Luke 24:47). This commission was to be carried out in the strength provided from heaven.

The next volume (Acts), also dedicated to Theophilus, records what Jesus continues to do and teach through his church by the enabling Holy Spirit's power. The book of Acts reemphasizes the aim of the Christ, the aid of the Spirit and the acts of the Missionaries. "Missionaries" is the Latin term for the Greek word "Apostles." They both mean "the ones sent."

Jesus' concern for the unevangelized, so apparent in the four Gospels, is the compelling thrust behind this New Testament book as well. In our present arrangement of the New Testament books, Acts has been placed between the Gospels and the Epistles. Following the Gospels, Acts shows how the disciples of Christ carried out his marching orders. Preceding the Epistles, it tells how the gospel reached many of the distant areas to which Christian letters would be written.

In the opening chapter of Acts, when the commissioned apostles are distracted by a *when* question ("Lord, are you at this time going to restore the kingdom to Israel?" [1:6]), Jesus brings them back by the *where* mission he had just given them ("You will be witnesses in Jerusalem, and in all Judea and Samaria, and to the ends of the earth" [1:8]). Until time is no more, the Christian mission of reaching all men should keep the church focused on the divine assignment of world evangelism and away from the human folly of prophetic date-setting.

How can twelve pebbles dropped in the ocean produce ripples effecting the far distant shores? How can twelve men start in Jerusalem and reach the world with their message? Jesus' clarifying answer is, "You will receive power when the Holy Spirit comes on you."

J.B. Phillips, in the introduction to his translation of the book of Acts, wrote, "These early Christians were led by the Holy Spirit to the main task of bringing people to God through Christ, and were not permitted to enjoy fascinating side tracks." Luke in Acts will present the Holy Spirit as the director of our mission, as his Gospel had introduced us to Jesus, as the founder of that mission.

As Luke's second volume begins, the giving of the Great Commission has been reviewed (1:1-11), the workers prepare themselves by prayer (1:12-14) and the apostolic band is brought back up to the full number of twelve (1:15-26), ready for witness as the birthday of the church is about to arrive with the Holy Spirit's coming. At the point of Pentecost, A. D. 30, the acts of the missionaries (the Acts of the Apostles) begin. The efforts of Peter and the Twelve are highlighted in the first portion of the scroll (Acts 1-12), while Paul's outreach becomes the stress in the latter section (Acts 13-28). J.C. O'Neill affirms that Luke "had the burning inner purpose of bringing men to the faith. . . . The repeated and dramatic demonstration that Christianity was both politically innocent and religiously the true fulfillment of the expectations of Judaism was not a legal but an evangelistic argument."[1] This is what one would expect from a coworker of Paul, the greatest missionary of all time.

Recording the Missionary Movements

Like a careful historian, Luke traces the spread of Christianity from Jerusalem (the center of Judaism) to Rome (the center of the world empire). He would not have us consider the church a Jewish sect, but a world-encircling kingdom. The key verse of Acts 1:8 schedules the gospel to be heard in the city ("Jerusalem"), the nation ("Judea and Samaria") and the world ("the ends of the earth"), just as Christ had ordered in the final chapter of Luke's Gospel ("all nations, beginning at Jerusalem" [Luke 24:47]).

The church's march, at first, is northward from Jerusalem (1:1-6:7), through Palestine and Samaria (6:8-9:31), to Antioch (9:32-12:24). From Antioch, under Paul's leadership, the gospel travels westward through Asia Minor (12:25-16:5) and Europe (16:6-19:20) to Rome (19:21-28:31).

Luke would have the readers catch the compulsion of the saved to reach every person and place yet unreached by salvation's story.

He would also have them rejoice in the missionary success accounts. These victory statements he can give about most every place where he tells of the workers going. New Testament scholars find six movements of outreach capped with a success claim. How did it go in Jerusalem? "The word of God spread. The number of disciples in Jerusalem increased rapidly, and a large number of priests became obedient to the faith" (6:7). Was there equal victory on the national scale? "The church throughout Judea, Galilee and

---

[1]J.C. O'Neill, *The Theology of Acts in Its Historical Setting* (London: SPCK, 1961), pp. 176, 180.

Samaria enjoyed a time of peace. It was strengthened; and encouraged by the Holy Spirit, it grew in numbers" (9:31). What was the reading on acceptance in Phoenicia and Syria? "The word of God continued to increase and spread" (12:24). Is the record upbeat regarding the Cyprus and Galatian effort? "The churches were strengthened in the faith and grew daily in numbers" (16:5). Was it still good news after striving for the gospel in Macedonia, Achaia and Asia? "The word of the Lord spread widely and grew in power" (19:20). Reaching the city of Rome with Paul in chains, has our author finally found defeat to have won out over victory? "For two whole years Paul stayed there in his own rented house and welcomed all who came to see him. Boldly and without hindrance he preached the kingdom of God and taught about the Lord Jesus Christ" (28:30-31).

Interspersed with these six passages, that follow the half-dozen geographical spreads of the message, are other shouts of victory in the face of all the difficulties that accompany the missionary thrust. On the first day of the church, "Those who accepted the message were baptized, and about three thousand were added to their number" (2:41) and soon this increasing enrollment was happening "daily" (2:47) until "the number of men grew to about five thousand" (4:4). The growth was not limited to men, as "more and more men and women believed in the Lord and were added to their number" (5:14). "The number of disciples was increasing" (6:1) and "many people believed in the Lord" (9:42). On some occasions, it could be reported that "almost the whole city gathered to hear the word of the Lord" (13:44). On other days, the diary of Luke could say, "They spoke so effectively that a great number of Jews and Gentiles believed" (14:1). Even after what could be called bloody battles, the Doctor traveling with Paul dips his pen in an inkwell of excitement and happiness, writing, "They received the message with great eagerness and examined the Scriptures every day to see if what Paul said was true. Many of the Jews believed, as did also a number of prominent Greek women and many Greek men" (17:11-12). "Thousands of Jews have believed" (21:20) are not the words of a discouraged missionary.

Providence had prepared the field for the planting of the gospel seed. Rome's control of the Mediterranean world led to the *Pax Romana*. Rome's military, with all its faults, meant the times were stable. Rome's roads, well built and maintained, allowed Christian messengers to travel freely most any direction. God, earlier, through the conquests of Alexander the Great, had made the single language of Greek a common tongue spoken everywhere. It was into the Greek language that the Old Testament had been translated and placed into libraries across the world. When everything was ready, God created the church and gave it His mission.

A century ago, a believer named Fitchett described the phenomenon we call the foreign missionary. His complimentary words were: "He has the scantiest equipment, he carries no arms, he is clad with no civil authority, he has very little money, he has only a message and a motive, but he works a miracle which science, literature, civilization cannot do — he creates a moral character in a people foul with the vices of heathenism. . . . Missions are the credentials of Christianity; they do not only diffuse Christianity, they prove it."[2]

As Luke records the missionary movements of the church of our Lord during its first three decades, he does not intend Rome to be the gospel's final destination. The final chapters on the world mission of Christ are still being written. A long-standing hermeneutical principle in the church has been that Christ's people in every time should do and believe that for which in the New Testament we can find either Divine command, Apostolic example or necessary inference. In regard to fulfilling the Great Commission, we have all three.

When military forces leave home for foreign battlefields, supporters are sometimes heard to cry out "Give 'em hell,

---

[2]Source unknown

boys." It is when Christ's army, with an altogether different order, leaves for the spiritual battle against paganism of every sort, backers always give the encouraging word, "Give 'em Christ, boys." Archibald McLean, recognizing the church as Christ's army, reminded believers that "An army exists for one and only one purpose. . . . An army has its drill ground, its target practice, its dress parade, its barracks, its colours. But an army does not exist for the drill ground or the target practice or the dress parade or the barracks. An army exists to fight when the nation wants fighting done."[3] Luke's Acts is boot camp for any soul-winner preparing for service. Luke's Acts is the army manual to be mastered in detail by each Christian soldier who puts on the uniform of Christ.

Recording the Missionary Message

The book before us does not alone trace the road maps and sea lanes followed by the first century missioners; it further puts in writing the gist of their messages. Nearly one-third of Acts is the content of the message that was being proclaimed when the church was young. Samples of Peter's sermons are found in Chapters 2, 3 and 10. Those of Paul are in Chapters 13, 17 and 20. Compare these with the messages coming from Stephen, the first Christian martyr (Chapter 7), or Philip, an early deacon (Chapter 8), and the missionary heart of the gospel is apparent.

A half dozen main points stand out. 1. The Old Testament forecasts of the last days are finding fulfillment (3:18). 2. Jesus, the promised Messiah from David's lineage, has been ministering miraculously in Israel (2:22-31). 3. His atoning death by crucifixion has been followed by resurrection, ascension and coronation (2:32-33). 4. The gift of the Holy

---

[3]Archibald McLean, *Where the Book Speaks* (New York: Fleming H. Revell Company, 1907), p. 35.

Spirit from heaven gives evidence of Jesus' glorification (2:33). 5. One day Jesus will return as the world's judge (3:21). 6. In response to God's actions in Christ, all believers are to repent and be immersed; for God has covenanted to remove the guilty person's sins and replace them with His holy presence upon this public signing-up ceremony of baptism, the Lord has prescribed (2:38).

The missionary messages, as preserved in the twenty-eight chapters of this book, hold before us the model for all soul-winners to follow. Each presentation of the *kerygma* had a trinity of traits worthy of our following when we present the gospel. One of the characteristics of proclamation was that they only talked about Jesus (8:35). No side concerns were allowed to bedim the main issue. Even Christ's moral teachings and miraculous powers took second place to the prime position reserved for the cross and resurrection of the Savior. A further quality in the apostolic sermons is the element of rich promises. The evangelists in Acts stressed the evangel of what God had accomplished through Jesus' conquest of sin through his passion and his victory over death by his resurrection. These historic events resulted in the gifts God would now bestow on all who accept them. Forgiveness is a gift. The Holy Spirit is a gift. Reception into God's family is a gift. Adoption, reconciliation or eternal life are gifts of grace on God's part; not the rewards of merit deserved on our part. The third of the triune traits in New Testament sermons is openly evident in messages by Peter, Paul or any other herald of the gospel. It was their call for decision.

Bible preachers did not give a nice talk to be followed by a benediction. What was anticipated was not a string of worshipers leaving the occasion while complimenting the spokesman for his uplifting meditation or his lambast against society's ills. Each speaker's intention was to make converts to Christ. Be the listener a full-blooded practicing Jew, in the holy city, a proselyte in a distant synagogue, or a Gentile far removed from Old Testament ways and lands, the story of

God's love demanded a verdict. Decision for, or decision against Christ was called for without timidity or hesitation. Since God had done so much for man, and had done so at such a price, straddling the fence was not an acceptable option.

In the cases of Peter and Paul, we see the apostles were more than simply heralds of facts or promises written for them to deliver. They were witnesses. That means their hearers were facing men of experience, not just hearsay. A.T. Pierson builds on this vital distinction:

> A herald is only the mouth of a message; a witness is the mouth of an experience. The public crier may announce or proclaim, for hire, tidings in which he feels no interest, and the truth of which he has no knowledge. But a witness can speak only what he knows and can testify what he has seen, heard, or felt. He is a herald, indeed, and a herald of good tidings, but he is more — he is an example and proof of their verity and value.[4]

None of us today can be a witness in the same sense as the Twelve or Paul. Those Apostles saw and heard the risen Christ to become the official witnesses to his resurrection event. But all successful missionary presentations of the gospel must come from the lips and lives of men and women who have experienced the forgiveness of their sins and the indwelling presence of Christ's Spirit. The world longs to hear of God's forgiveness from one who has been forgiven. It yearns for fellowship in a family of supportive love, where the spokespersons radiate the compassion of which they speak. The church grew in the years that Luke records, because transformed lives, glowing hope and loving actions had their appeal to common people everywhere. The same words of grace told by gracious Christians in today's world have their attraction in our time as well.

---

[4]Paul G. Alley, *The Missionary Enterprise Unit VII* (Wheaton: Evangelical Teacher Training Association, 1962), p. 3.

Recording the Missionary Methods

New methods for today are worth trying, if it can be shown that they work. But old, tried and true ways of converting the lost are not to be neglected. They brought great results in the opening days of Christian history and will still be effective until the Lord comes. We are grateful to Luke for his records of Paul's methodologies. They are worthy of consideration by modern strategists in missions.

From the record of Acts 13-28, one gets the impression that Paul designed to take the gospel to one Roman province after another until the job was fulfilled or death called for a halt. Reading and rereading the chapters of Acts deepens the conviction that the former persecutor of believers, now has a master plan that programs the establishment of Christian outposts in all the main centers of the Roman world. Charles L. Slattery is correct in saying, "Missions is the church in love with the whole world." Paul exemplifies that love. No place is to be without the church's message. No person is to be left without witness to the Savior. In a world crammed with optional demands for our time and attention, the missionary of all missionaries, calls us to let world evangelism receive the priority it deserves.

The book of Acts is a book of missionary records. Those records have been preserved by the Holy Spirit to be read and adopted by each succeeding generation. To follow Paul on each missionary journey is to see him target a large population center — a major city (like Antioch or Corinth) or a prominent leader (Sergius Paulus or Herod Agrippa). No person in the hinterland is less worthy of the message, but establishing a work in Ephesus or Thessalonica is to leave a mission outpost to radiate the story far and wide from its location. Converts of the missionaries are to carry out the mission as well. Winning leaders assures that those who follow leaders will follow them into the kingdom.

A congregation of the redeemed on the Lord's day was a

gathering for instruction and strength. The dispersion of the gathered flock was but a dismissal to the opportunities of both witnessing to and serving the millions among which each individual lived. These gatherings were often in homes, like those of Jason, Lydia, Philemon and others. These basic units of society became the basic unit in the Church's growth. Mary's home in Jerusalem, Philip's house in Caesarea or your residence in the modern world can be a place for Bible study, prayer and outreach to the community.

This home-centered evangelism gives credence to the observation of E.M. Bliss, regarding missionaries in New Testament days: "Of missionaries in the modern sense of the term, there were few; but of those who made their trade, their profession, their everyday occupation, of whatever sort, the means of extending their faith, there was a multitude."[5]

On Paul's priority list was the technique of "to the Jew first." This strategy called for starting with the people easiest to begin with. Synagogues were almost everywhere. Jews were the people of the book. At every Sabbath gathering, readings from the Law and the Prophets would be followed by opportunities for a visiting Jew to comment on the text. Since the coming Messiah was the burden of the Ancient Scriptures, Paul found endless opportunities to open the meaning of the familiar texts with evidence that Jesus fulfilled those hopes and dreams.

Another methodology of the Apostle to the Gentiles was to revisit the congregations he had started. Often before he would head west to virgin territory, he can be found confirming in the faith the new converts of an earlier mission. An encouraging voice held people to their newly-founded hopes. A confirming pen wrote to persons and congregations needing continuing support for their convictions.

Let those who would put their hands to the task of reaching for the lost in Christ's name bathe themselves in this

---

[5]E.M. Bliss, *The Missionary Experience* (New York: Fleming H. Revell, 1908), p. 12.

missionary handbook called Acts. The persons that walk across the stage of the world do open-air preaching to masses and one-on-one conversing with a traveler in his chariot. A beggar at the temple gate, or a Roman official with house guests at a feast, become the audience fortunate to hear the story of salvation.

We can draw no less conclusion than that Luke is more than a historian interested in some ancient facts. Hebrew culture in the capital of the Jewish world is not his interest. The conversion of the whole world, from the capital city of Judaism is his burden. The reading of his document has for twenty centuries kept reminding the church why it is here.

CHAPTER 7

Reaching for the City
Acts 1-6

The first five years of Christian history found the Twelve proclaiming Christ in the city of Jerusalem. It was there Jesus had been crucified. It was there he had risen from the dead. It was there for forty days many of his post-resurrection appearances to his Apostles had occurred to remove any doubt as to the fact of his being alive.

In the city where the gospel events had happened — not thousands of miles distant where checking out the claims would be next to impossible — the church was born. It was on an early Sunday morning. The Christ, who had conquered the grave on a Sunday seven weeks prior, poured out his Holy Spirit on the twelve witnesses we call the Apostles. In relating the happening of that Pentecost day, Luke describes "a sound like the blowing of a violent wind" and a visual display of "what seemed to be tongues of fire that separated and came to rest on each of them" (2:2-3). What a fitting symbol for God's messengers, ready to fulfill their mission as witnesses with flaming tongues. Just as a Kansas or Oklahoma wheat field after harvest will likely be burned over, so the world was to become the area where the gospel flame was to burn, leaving no corner of the field untouched. "Fire" suggests the zeal which was to accompany the apostolic witness. "Tongues" describe the way the story will be made known.

At the end of Luke's report of the Christian effort in this urban center of Judaism, is the report of evangelistic success: "So the word of God spread. The number of disciples increased rapidly, and a large number of priests became obedient to the faith" (6:7). Before we leave this meaningful verse and spend time considering from this section of Acts how to win cities for Christ, do not miss two significant truths in the final phrase of this summary passage.

Note the last four words: "obedient to the faith." No unnatural separation here of faith and action, no suggesting that one only believe, there is nothing required to do. Paul, the known advocate of justification by faith, spoke of judgment falling, not alone on disbelievers, but also on those who "do not obey the gospel of our Lord Jesus" (2 Thess. 1:8). "Believe the gospel" is not a suggestive command that removes "obey the gospel." A scan reading, regarding the Old Testament heroes of faith enumerated in Hebrews chapter eleven, gives evidence that in each incident obedience to divine command is what is described correctly as "faith."

Now also pay heed to Acts 6:7's final line that those obeying the faith included "a large number of priests." The evangelistic significance of this statement is not to be missed. Win to Jesus an average person and all heaven rejoices. But win a "priest," or a host of "priests," and an even greater consequence will follow. Religious leaders in turning to the faith bring many of those who have respected them to the same decision. Those priests, who spent much of their lives in sacrificing innocent lambs as substitutes for sin-guilty people, found in Jesus the Lamb that God himself had provided.

The lesson is to pray for, and seek to win for Jesus, every person with whom you come in contact; but do not hesitate, because of timidity, to share the Lord with leaders. They have the same spiritual needs as other people. Cast your line into the sea of humanity, praying that occasionally God will grant you a big fish that in turn will attract the other fish in the sea.

Winning by Learning the City's Languages (Acts 2)

As Acts 6:7 reports the closing results of the Jerusalem endeavor, Acts 2:1-13 describes the opening scene. The prior promise of Christ to his Apostles, that they would in a few days "be baptized with the Holy Spirit" (1:5) to empower their witness (1:8), finds fulfillment, when on Pentecost, "All of them were filled with the Holy Spirit and began to speak in other tongues as the Spirit enabled them" (2:4).

Whoever sets out to win an urban center for Jesus, at once confronts a situation demanding ability to communicate the gospel to the populace of many dialects. Each prospective convert is only capable of grasping the story if it is spoken in words with which that human is familiar. It is not unusual today to find in city centers a Korean speaking congregation, a Cambodian Bible class or a Vietnamese group worshiping in the same building as an English speaking church. The universal body language of love is evident between them all as they meet and greet; but, until a common language is learned, the sermons must be in the language familiar to the listener.

Today a missionary headed for Japan will strive to master Japanese. One hoping to target Mexican-Americans in the Southwest will work at becoming fluent in Spanish. In the initial years of the early church, a special miraculous gift from the Holy Spirit enabled the Apostles (who were all Galilean) to fulfill their commission without taking years of study in foreign languages. That same "gift of tongues" was shared on new mission fields with others so that the mission could get off to a good start.

Acts 2:4 is the first use in this book by Luke of the word "tongues." Being the first mention of the term, it is clearly defined so that Theophilus and the other readers will know what the described phenomenon is. Verses 5-12 constitute his definition. The phrases "his own language," or "his own native language," or "our own tongues" seem to tell of a miraculous gift for the missionaries as they communicated the story of Christ to "Parthians, Medes and Elamites; residents of Mesopotamia, Judea and Cappadocia, Pontus and Asia, Phrygia and Pamphylia, Egypt and the parts of Lybia near Cyrene; visitors from Rome . . . Cretans and Arabs" (2:9-11). The city of Jerusalem on that day had much in common with a Los Angeles or New York in our time.

The city where you live is a place filled with foreign missionary opportunity. The Watchman magazine told many years ago of a girl who had prayed for God to make her a foreign missionary. The periodical relates an imaginary conversation that the heavenly Father had with her:

"Sophia, where were you born?" "In Germany." "Where are you now?" "America." "Then you are a foreign missionary already. Who lives on the floor above your apartment?" "A family of Swedes." "And who dwells on the floor above that, the apartment to the rear and the house around the corner?" "There are Switzers above, Italians in back and a Chinese family around the block." At this point God is said to have remarked, "You have never spoken a word to these people about my Son! Do you think I will send you thousands of miles to foreigners, when you never care enough about those near your own door?"

Acts 2 is a word picture of any major city needing the story of Jesus. There will be persons "from every nation under heaven" (2:5). They all need to hear of God's love for the unlovely. It is up to the creative "downtown church" to find a way to communicate heaven's glad tidings to the multiple groups that constitute the city. Peter is right in quoting Joel's revelation of God's desire for these last days to "pour out [his] Spirit on all people" (2:17). The enablement, to preach at once in the needed language of each moment, was Christ's gift to his Apostles (his Missionaries). The Spirit's outpouring was not to make them feel great, but to enable them to fulfill his great commission. When the task is to witness to others, the personal experience of ecstacy is a poor substitute. When the assignment is to make clear the gospel, ecstatic speech uninterpreted misses the mark.

The content of the story that the apostles told is the burden of most of the Acts 2 chapter. As those baptized believers "devoted themselves to the apostles' (missionaries') teaching" (2:42), let modern city-dwellers, who know the Savior, also take to the streets and marketplaces with the same facts, commands and promises. The correct response to the offer of grace will not vary country by country, nor decade by decade. The promise tied to faith, repentance and baptism on that initial day of the church was for them and theirs, plus "all whom the Lord our God will call" (2:38-39). I. Howard Marshall recognizes Luke's purpose behind both his Gospel and his Acts of the Apostles, writing, "It was enough that he should compose this record as a means of evangelism."[1]

Winning by Healing the City's Hurts (Acts 3)

In reaching the Holy Cities of some Jerusalem, Rome or Mecca, there will be the requirement of learning languages so communication can take place. In reaching the not-so-holy cities that dot today's maps of the world, there also will be the necessity of healing the multiplicity of hurts that are on many of the street corners and behind many of the bolted doors.

Shortly after the "three thousand" conversions in the city following Peter's first gospel sermon (2:41), "the number of men grew to about five thousand" (4:5). One significant contributing factor was the continuing healing ministry of Jesus through his witnesses (5:12).

A beggar, who from birth had been hurting as a cripple,

---

[1]I. Howard Marshall, *Luke: Historian and Theologian* (Grand Rapids: Zondervan, 1970), p. 221.

found Peter and John not leaving him with a small dole to continue his life of misery for another day. These representatives of Jesus gave him more than he ever dreamed. Through faith in the Lord came complete and immediate restoration of health, which had been missing for forty years. The total transformation of one, who had to be "carried" (3:2) and had to spend each day as a beggar, into a worshiper "walking and praising God" (3:9), was a living demonstration of what Christ could do for "all peoples of earth" (3:25).

The lesson for every modern urbanite is that all cities have people that hurt. When today's disciples of the Great Physician see needs through Jesus' eyes and care enough to reach out in love and lift the fallen up, respect is earned — the community notices — and formerly closed minds are readied to listen (3:11-26). Many growing congregations this hour are doing the same. Their philosophy is find a need and fill it. Do working parents need day-care help for their little ones? Do recovering alcoholics or dope addicts need a support group? Is there life after divorce or after loss of a job? Classes for singles or small home study groups, or — you name it — the list is endless — are started to meet real needs. Find a hurt and heal it. Find a lonesome widow or a withdrawn teenager. Find a young boy who is never selected for a ball team. Figure a way to make the hurt individual your friend and soon he or she will find Jesus as the best friend anyone can have. The hurting man in Acts 3 was at the gate of the temple. The person crying for help in your town is apt to be right outside the door of your church house.

Winning by Overcoming the City's Resistance (Acts 4)

Speaking the language of the populace and healing the hurts of individuals does not only bring large numbers into the kingdom; it usually brings on strong resistance from other quarters. Jesus went about doing good and the Scribes and Pharisees were upset that the common people heard Jesus gladly. Now his new-formed church is blessing all and harming none, but priests and Sadducees seize and imprison Peter and John. That means jail and threats. That brings the fright-producing words, "Warn these men to speak no longer to anyone in this name [of Christ]" (4:17).

Loud harangue and manifestations of force could not silence those Christ had commissioned to speak. He who has all authority (Matt. 28:18) had said "make disciples." Now political entities and religious parties are attempting to muzzle the message and its messengers. The Christian response is courage and prayer. Valor speaks in unquivering voice and unyielding will, "We cannot help speaking about what we have seen and heard" (4:20). Unbowed backs before civil hierarchies, but bended knees before the Sovereign Lord, lead to enabling intercession. The prayer of the persecuted is not for escape from pain nor deliverance from problems. No line of the group's prayers for heaven's ears is a request for escape. Each request is "enable your servants to speak . . . with great boldness" (4:29). The earthquake that follows is God's "Amen!" The result that ensues is that Spirit-filled men "spoke the word of God boldly" (4:31).

If today's city church will pray for the right thing, its prayers will also be answered. The needed intercession is not escape from the city with its problems and obstacles. It is prayer for boldness and the wisdom to share effectively the salvation "found in . . . no other name under heaven" (4:12). Some Christians have been sent to Siberia, others have run to Suburbia, but some others must stay in the inner city.

I read of a preacher who startled his congregation by announcing he planned to go on a mission to the heathen. At the end of the worship hour, members expressed astonishment at his leaving them. They begged to learn when and where he was going and what they were expected to do in his absence. His retort, was, "My good friends, to go on a mission to the heathen will not necessitate my leaving town."

Cities in America need Christ ever as much as those in Hindu, Moslem or Spiritist communities.

Problems were meant for solving, not escaping. Obstacles overcome in one locale give helpful hints to others in similar difficulties. When land cannot be found for building a gathering hall — when monies cannot be located for erecting an edifice for worship — when government groups throw roadblocks before all your plans, what should one do? With God's help find a new way and let that Spirit-directed solution become a help for other groups of disciples wrestling with the same dilemma. The one answer never to be given is dissolution. Quitting is not in the Christian's dictionary.

Winning by Multiplying the Church's Ministry (Acts 4:32-6:6)

What some call obstacles, others term opportunities. That earliest Jerusalem church met needs by multiplying ministries. Was there hunger? Then love's response will be sharing. When "all the believers . . . shared everything they had," the evangelistic consequence was bound to be that "with great power the apostles continued to testify to the resurrection of the Lord Jesus" (5:32-33).

The flickering candles of Ananias and Sapphira catch the eye. But do not let the wavering of two church people in greed, cause you to miss the steady light glowing in the rest of the faithful membership. "All the believers were one in heart and mind. . . . There were no needy persons among them" (4:32,34). This is a compliment to the moral majority. Like Barnabas, the many were willing to sell assets and donate the proceeds to relieve human need (4:36-37).

No one member of Christ's body can meet the vast cries for help that are heard everywhere. But, as a caring family, each can do a part until the little from the many becomes enough to accomplish the task. A particular congregation of Christ's people may be defined as a small church. Yet, when

Christ is present, the little becomes a lot. As surely as Jesus could bless the five small loaves and the two little fish of a young lad until multitudes were adequately fed, God's blessing on the freewill gifts of the few gathered in his name becomes sufficient to do the needed work.

With every believer giving out of his pool of assets, work is done in the city that could never be accomplished by any individual alone. The generous hearts of the many win victories, because monetary giving is joined with healing hands. "The apostles performed many miraculous signs and wonders among the people" (5:12). These men to whom Jesus promised such awesome power (Matt. 10:1-8), demonstrated visibly Christ's gospel of saving power. Unlike the many pretenders of our day, who claim equal status with the apostles of the first century, these genuine witnesses to Christ's resurrection turned no sick individual away. For, of the many carried to Peter or another of the Twelve, "all of them were healed" (5:16). No one was sent home disappointed, or rebuked for lack of faith. No wonder "more and more men and women believed in the Lord and were added to their number" (5:14).

For long centuries the missionaries going to pagan cities with the gospel, have preached the love of God accompanied by outward demonstration of that love. It is not unusual to read of a missionary to India opening an eye clinic, or of a foreign messenger to Thailand building a hospital to minister to the sick in Jesus' name. In Africa the gospel spokesman may open a school, so the new believers can become literate and follow the Bible's teaching. In Japan or Okinawa it may be a leprosarium that grows out of the Christian teacher's love for the sick. The main product must be gospel proclamation. Still, by-products of blessing come as an extra dividend where Christ is known.

The church is a family of many children — a body of many members. Each person is a part of the team. Some give (cp. 4:32-5:11), some help in the healing ministries (5:12-16) and others share at the witnessing task (5:17-42). God's angel freed the apostles from jail with the assignment, "Go, stand in the temple courts . . . tell the people the full message of this new life" (5:19-20). The heavenly order was so gladly obeyed that the Sanhedrin objected, "We gave you strict orders not to teach in this name. . . . Yet you have filled Jerusalem with your teaching" (5:28). God would be pleased if the modern city congregations had the same charge hurled at them. The threat will always be there. It may come from a Gestapo officer or an A.C.L.U. lawyer. It will likely command "not to speak in the name of Jesus" (5:40). The response will ever be the same from God's children. Today, as then, the missionary record will read, "Day after day, in the temple courts and from house to house, they never stopped teaching and proclaiming the good news that Jesus is the Christ" (5:42).

Generous hearts, healing hands, witnessing lips and new ministries make for a quartet of efforts to reach a city. Acts 6:1-6 describes the need in Jerusalem created by the growing size of the membership. The numerical increase demanded a division of labor. Twelve preachers must not "neglect the ministry of the word of God in order to wait on tables" (6:2). It would be wiser to have others tend to the benevolent-care side of the Christian work, freeing the missionaries to give attention "to prayer and the ministry of the word" (6:4). Church work is not to be a one-man show. No "clergyman" is to be the only minister in a gathered flock. Every Christian is in the ministry. No one person in a single church can hope to win a city, much less the surrounding countryside. That will take the Biblical understanding of the priesthood of all believers.

Our twentieth and twenty-first century world is, and will remain, more urban than rural. There are lessons by the Holy Spirit in city evangelism preserved in the opening chapters of Luke's missionary history. If we learn the many languages, strive to heal the many hurts and refuse to be overcome by the resistance that is bound to be there in a world under Satan's domination, we can place Christ's banner over the metropolitan centers of the globe. Multiplying the hands of workers is crucial to success. In your congregation see that every person finds his place of ministry. The preachers or elders are not to do the work of one hundred people. It would be better to inspire a hundred persons to work.

CHAPTER 8

Reaching for the Nation
Acts 7-9

Luke's historical record of church expansion is: first the city, then the nation and ultimately the world. The key verse of Acts 1:8 named "Jerusalem . . . all Judea and Samaria" and "the ends of the earth." At the conclusion of the report, on the second step of this plan, Luke rejoices that "the church throughout Judea, Galilee and Samaria enjoyed a time of peace . . . it grew in numbers" (9:31).

The material, included in this "national" section, centers around three persons — Stephen, Philip and Saul. The reason our author tells of the selection of the seven (6:5) that we call deacons is because two of that number (Stephen and Philip) are pivotal characters in the mission-outreach story. The harshest opponent of the church, Saul of Tarsus, witnesses with approval the stoning of Stephen. This event likely is a contributing factor to Paul's conversion from persecutor of believers to their most ardent advocate, as detailed in Acts 9.

Stephen: Christ's Messenger, Martyr and Mirror

Immediately following the summary verse that concluded the Jerusalem report (6:7), Stephen the "deacon" is introduced as "a man full of God's grace and power" who "did great wonders and miraculous signs among the people" (6:8).

Prior to the laying on of the hands of the Apostles upon the seven, we only know of miracles being "done by the apostles" (2:43; 5:12). But, from the ordination as servants of the Jerusalem church, charismatic gifts (such as healing and wisdom) seem to extend to the workers selected by the congregation but set apart by the apostolic band.

Such divine aid brought the result that Jews who "began to argue with Stephen . . . could not stand up against his wisdom or the Spirit by whom he spoke" (16:10). The false charges leveled against the church are that Christians are "against Moses . . . against God" (6:11) and against the "holy place" (6:13). The first complaint, "against Moses," is also worded, "against the law," for it was Moses that had given God's law to Israel.

In Stephen's response to the three charges, he gives clear and convincing refutation. Acts 7:2-19 belies the accusation of being anti-God. The opposite is true. Verses 20-43 show the falsity of the charge of being anti-Moses and anti-law. As to the insinuation that a Christian is anti-temple, verses 44-50 ought to stop that sham idea. The speech by Stephen concludes with the allegation that the Jewish opponents are "stiff-necked people, with uncircumcised hearts and ears," implying that they indeed received God's law but do not obey it (7:51-53).

In the rest of the seventh chapter, the messenger becomes the martyr and the mirror. Stephen is the first of a long train of individuals who will be called upon to give their lives for the Christ they preach. If the enemies of Jesus despise hearing about the Christ of the cross, covering "their ears and yelling at the top of their voices" (7:57), they will see the Savior mirrored before them in the way Stephen dies. His actions speak the gospel as loudly as his words.

Did Jesus, being tortured in his crucifixion, call out to God, "Father, into your hands I commit my spirit" (Luke 23:46)? Then catch the glimpse of the church's first martyr, being stoned for his testimony, praying aloud, "Lord Jesus, receive my spirit" (7:59). Did the Man of Galilee show love for those nailing him to the rood; saying, "Father, forgive them, for they do not know what they are doing" (Luke 23:34)? Then listen as Stephen intercedes for his tormentors, while the rocks crush out his life, praying, "Lord, do not hold this sin against them" (7:60). Both the stoning of Stephen and the crucifixion of Jesus took place "out of the city" (7:58 cp. Heb. 13:12). Christlikeness is the *sine qua non* of missionary outreach. A life changed, to the way of acting and thinking like Jesus, is the strongest evidence to the gospel's truth.

One could only wish that the gospel's spread from the city of Jerusalem outward to the rest of Israel and the world was because his followers took seriously the words of Jesus' *great* commission. The information in Acts attributes the geographic extension, rather, to the "*great* persecution" that broke out "against the church at Jerusalem." Luke states the fact that "all except the apostles were scattered throughout Judea and Samaria" (8:3).

Philip: Christ's Public and Personal Evangelist

At this point, another of the Jerusalem church's seven ministers, or servants, is featured in Luke's story of how the gospel spread. Following his usual technique of naming a general truth and then following that with a specific illustration of that truth, Luke begins, "Those who had been scattered preached the word everywhere they went" (8:4). With the principle stated, that all those Christians driven out of Jerusalem spread the word about Christ, Luke uses Philip as an example of what each of those scattered persons is doing. He writes, "Philip went down to a city in Samaria and proclaimed the Christ there . . . they all paid close attention" (8:5-6).

As believers are running for their lives and seeking homes in which to stay, those host families are certain to ask why they were there and what forced them out of their houses. This led to multiple opportunities to tell about Jesus of Nazareth who had been crucified by men but resurrected by God. The message delivered was Christ centered. No side issues are raised to befuddle the minds over sectarian dogmas or party tenets. They have one story to tell. Like Philip, they tell only "the good news about Jesus" (8:35). Another way to describe their message is to say that they "preached the good news of the kingdom of God and the name of Jesus Christ" (8:12), or they "proclaimed the word of the Lord . . . preaching the gospel" (9:25,40).

In telling the facts, Philip and the others also make clear the great commission's specified response of baptism. So, wherever Philip preaches in Samaria, "they were baptized, both men and women" (8:13). This "deacon" of the local congregation in Jerusalem can no longer serve in that capacity while he is miles away from the church that selected him for that role. He becomes "Philip the evangelist" (21:8).

In his public "preaching the gospel in all the towns until he reached Caesarea" (8:40), Philip calls the penitents to be "baptized, both men and women" (8:12). This was in harmony with the apostles', "Repent and be baptized" (2:38) spoken on the first day of the church. Yet the soul-winner, who speaks to groups about Jesus, also spends time with individuals as a personal evangelist. The account of the Ethiopian eunuch, which Luke relates, tells of Philip hitching a chariot ride under the Spirit's direction. Explaining the Messianic prophecy of Isaiah 53, the preacher "began with that very passage of Scripture and told him the good news about Jesus" (8:35).

It comes as no surprise that one, who hears only the story "about Jesus," would ask to be baptized. The eunuch heard of Jesus' ministry commencing when he was baptized by John, and concluding with his great commission promise that "Whoever believes and is baptized will be saved" (Mark 16:16). So hearing only the message of Christ and responding, as all converts of the Bible days did, "both Philip and the eunuch went down into the water and Philip baptized him" (8:38).

Luke remembers how responsive Philip was to the Holy Spirit's instruction, "Go to that chariot" (8:29). He writes, "Then Philip ran" (8:30). For our nation, which seems to be slipping from the high ideal present at the nation's founding, we need soul-winners who will *run* to the lost. For too long we have straggled behind at the evangelism task. Robert Shaw of Miami, Florida, in a sermon over twenty years ago, quoted Jesse Wilson stating, "Christians have lost the word 'urgency.' We have not been in a hurry for so long that even when we sing 'O Zion Haste!' we drag the tempo."

Both the Jewish nation of Judea, Samaria and Galilee and our nation of fifty states need the gospel quickly. It is time for believers to *run* with the message of hope. The eunuch was from distant Ethiopia. The Samaritans were half-breeds. But that could not detour a follower of the Master Teacher who stated that our Heavenly Father loves prodigals even in "a distant country" (Luke 15:13). Any nation with its cultural or racial mix is on God's priority list for hearing of salvation through His Son.

Paul: Past Persecutor and Present Preacher

Acts 9 is the first of three Lukan accounts of Paul's conversion (Acts 22 and 26). The first account is told in Luke's second section, dealing with the gospel's spread throughout the nation. The mission work of Paul will be the highlight of Acts 13-28, but his point of conversion contributes to the success of the national effort earlier. Luke pens that because this rabid opponent of the cross ceased his anti-church activity, "Then the church throughout Judea, Galilee and Samaria enjoyed a time of peace. It was strengthened and encouraged by the Holy Spirit, it grew in numbers, living in the fear of the Lord" (9:31).

There is no question that Paul had been a missionary of persecution on behalf of the Jewish Sanhedrin. He traveled far and wide, going beyond the borders of his nation even to Damascus in Syria. He scoured the synagogues, seeking men or women that he might make his prisoners, bringing them to Jerusalem for trial. Christ saw in this zealous person the quality he sought for his missionaries. The Lord longed for persons who would search the nations for men and women that could be made prisoners of the gospel, bringing them to Christ.

Paul's call to Apostleship was to make him Christ's "chosen instrument to carry [his] name before the Gentiles and their kings and before the people of Israel" (9:15). Being now an eyewitness that Jesus was alive after his passion, he knew that the church's story, which he so long had fought, was the truth. He would not need years of specialized training in a Christian apprenticeship to qualify him to teach. Rather in Damascus "at once he began to preach in the synagogues that Jesus is the Son of God" (9:20). He "grew more and more powerful and baffled the Jews living in Damascus by proving that Jesus is the Christ" (9:22).

Barnabas, who will later be Paul's partner in the missionary thrust into Cyprus and Galatia, earlier assures the Jerusalem disciples "how in Damascus he [Paul] had preached fearlessly in the name of Jesus" and in Jerusalem was "speaking boldly in the name of the Lord" both talking and debating "with the Grecian Jews" (9:27-29).

Saul of Tarsus, the special apostle to the Gentile world, is not one to go exclusively to Gentiles. "To the Jew first," is always his motto. The last half of Acts will trace the Apostle's work in the Gentile world (although, even there it will be to the Jew first). In the first half of the book, Luke wants us to see that Paul's testimony is also "before the people of Israel" (9:15). As convincing as was his reasoning from Scriptures, his transformed life, since the day he met Christ on the Damascus road, is the strongest evidence that he had seen

Jesus. His thinking is transformed. His emotions are on fire with the message of hope for all people. His will is bent low before Jesus his Lord, anxious to carry out his orders of world conquest. His changed life, from emissary of Jewish priests with the mission of stopping the new faith, to captain of Christ's army, with the assignment of spreading the new story, is the miracle that proves his case.

We will win no nation, no city — not even a household — without the messengers of new birth being demonstrations of Jesus' transforming power. Stephen was a living example of a life changed into Christlikeness. So was Philip. So was Saul. So must we be. Christ's Holy Spirit within the missioner makes the message credible. Consistent holiness of life cannot be faked. By fruit, true disciples of Jesus are known.

CHAPTER 9

Reaching for the World
Acts 10-28

"The world is my parish," claimed John Wesley. "To the ends of the earth," (1:8) commanded Jesus Christ. "The city 'Yes,' the nation 'Certainly,' and the entire world, 'Absolutely,'" cries the obedient church. We must be neither too near-sighted nor too far-sighted in our mission effort, but ever clear-sighted in the light of Christ's instruction. Foreign missions or home missions are not options open to us, because no field is foreign to Christ. A local Christian congregation must be more than local in outlook, or it cannot claim to be a Christian church, since "Christian" implies following Jesus. Jerusalem *and* Judea *and* Samaria *and* the uttermost parts are concurrent orders, not consecutive ones.

God's purpose in history is to bring reconciliation through His Son to the lost world. The church's goal is identical to that of the Heavenly Father. Believers are the hands of Christ, reaching, on his behalf, to all mankind. Did Jesus come from heaven to earth "to seek and to save what was lost" (Luke 19:6)? Then the Son of Man is a cross-cultural missionary. He moved from Paradise on high to the foreign country of earth. His redemptive acts in Palestine were for the benefit of every nation.

The Gospel Goes to Phoenicia and Syria (9:32-12:24)

As Luke's missionary record gets ready to relate Paul's outreach to the Gentile world, Acts first needs to tell of the conversion of the first Gentiles — the household of Cornelius. Since Peter is to be the chosen vessel to open the door to the uncircumcision, as he had done earlier for the Jews in Acts 2, the latter part of Acts 9 (32-43) is simply detailing how the big fisherman gets to Caesarea, where Cornelius is stationed. Simon Peter is going on preaching tours out from Jerusalem. He ministers in Lydda. The healing there of Aeneas, the paralytic, leads to the happy outcome that "all those who lived in Lydda and Sharon saw him and turned to the Lord" (9:35). Next he labors in Joppa with the similar good result that "all over Joppa . . . many people believed in the Lord" (9:42). It was while he is in this community that the news of Cornelius' readiness to hear the gospel reaches his ears. He ends up in Caesarea where this Roman centurion, with his relatives and close friends, gather to hear God's good news.

The lesson from the vision, repeated three times, that Peter has experienced (with God instructing him to eat what he has always counted forbidden) shapes his opening remarks: "I now realize how true it is that God does not show favoritism but accepts men from every nation who fear him and do what is right" (10:34-35). The work of reaching out to the whole world will never be accomplished until that lesson is learned. The lesson is that God pours his Holy Spirit "even on the Gentiles" (10:45). When the incident is reported in Judea "that the Gentiles also had received the word of God" (11:1), there are not long-standing objections, but rather immediate rejoicing that "God has granted even the Gentiles repentance unto life" (11:18).

The breaking down of prejudicial barriers begins to happen in Phoenicia, Cyprus and Antioch where the message thus far has only reached Jewish ears. Yet, at about the same time as Cornelius' conversion, believers begin "to speak to

Greeks also telling them the good news about the Lord Jesus" (11:20). This unshackling of the gospel, allowing it to flow freely to non-Jews, has God's approval. The missionary record, which is the book of Acts, says, "The Lord's hand was with them, and a great number of people believed and turned to the Lord" (11:21) or "were brought to the Lord" (11:24), with the added designation that "the word of God continued to increase and spread" (12:24).

It seems fitting that the title "Christian" (11:26) is saved, until this point in missionary advance, to be given to Christ's followers. The word implies belonging to Christ. Now, with old prejudices and national pride evaporating, the church is beginning to look more truly like the Messiah they purport to follow.

The Gospel Goes to Cyprus and Galatia (12:25-16:5)

Since many biblical scholars believe Luke to have described the expansion of the Church in six sections of approximately five years each, at this point we are to the fourth missionary movement as we look at Barnabas and Saul being commissioned out of the Antioch congregation. The guiding Holy Spirit — the administrator of mission outreach — says, "Set apart for me Barnabas and Saul for the work to which I have called them" (13:2). Barnabas, being "a Levite from Cyprus" (4:36), has a special desire to let the gospel story be heard first by his kinsmen.

On Cyprus, from Seleucia, the port of debarkation, to Paphos, the port of embarkation toward Galatia, our preachers proclaim "the word of God in the Jewish synagogues" (13:5). The glad result is that even "the proconsul Sergius Paulus . . . wanted to hear the word of God" (13:7). What he sees and hears brings him to faith, "for he was amazed at the teaching about the Lord" (13:12).

To the north of the isle of Cyprus is the Roman province

of Galatia, with Antioch of Pisidia as the next spot for church planting. Using the synagogue as the starting place and the Sabbath days as the occasions for addressing gathered Jews, it could be claimed that "almost the whole city gathered to hear the word of the Lord" (13:44). The appearance of interest on the part of the Jewish populace brings strong opposition from zealous religious leaders, resulting in the gospel-flow turning toward the Gentile citizens of the area.

The spokesmen respond, "We had to speak the word of God to you first. Since you reject it . . . we now turn to the Gentiles. For this is what the Lord has commanded us: 'I have made you a light for the Gentiles, that you may bring salvation to the ends of the earth'" (13:46-47). Just as the principle, "Win a leader and you win the followers of the leader," is valid; so is the maxim, "Win a city and you influence the surrounding territory." Luke says as much in stating, "The word of the Lord spread through the whole region" (13:49).

Under expulsion, the workers head for the next major city of Galatia which is Iconium. There again is initial success with the report: "Paul and Barnabas went as usual into the Jewish synagogue. There they spoke so effectively that a great number of Jews and Gentiles believed" (14:1). Once again religious opponents divide the people of the city and devise a plot to stone the spokesmen. Still again the workers have to flee to the next communities (Lystra and Derbe) "where they continue to preach the good news" (14:6-7). Upon winning "a large number of disciples . . . they return to Lystra, Iconium and Antioch, strengthening the disciples and encouraging them" (14:21-22). They continue this pattern of returning to visit a formerly founded church. After the Jerusalem Conference and after teaching and preaching awhile in Antioch, Paul says to his partner, "Let us go back and visit the brothers in all the towns where we preached the word of the Lord and see how they are doing" (15:36). Again after Paul teams up with Silas instead of Barnabas for the next westward thrust, he goes "through Syria and Cilicia, strengthening the churches" (15:41).

The lessons for missionaries today jump out from these Sacred Pages. He who goes on a mission must have the quality of bravery. He needs to head for major centers and let his aim include some leading persons. The laborer must recognize that, having but one life to give for Christ, it ought to be used in the most fruitful way possible. Whenever the open doors come, leave behind a church. Revisit that congregation and strengthen it, so that from it may grow more churches of the same faith and practice. Return to the sending church, as Paul and Barnabas returned to Antioch "where they had been committed to the grace of God for the work they had now completed" (14:26). If the pair set aside by the laying on of hands in Acts 13 were foreign missionaries, then the sending congregation could call its members "Intercessory foreign missionaries." There would have been few victories to report had there not been prayer warriors sharing in the battles from the home base of Antioch in Syria.

The council, held at Jerusalem, and reported in Acts 15, is to manifest the unity of Peter, Paul and the Jerusalem church, in the face of potential disruption by Judaizers. It gives opportunity for leaders to show their unanimous agreement that the mission is meant to include Gentiles. Paul and Barnabas tell "how the Gentiles had been converted" (15:3). Peter reports, "God made a choice among you that the Gentiles might hear from my lips the message of the gospel and believe" (15:7). James, speaking for the Jerusalem congregation from which the troublemakers claimed to have received their authority, climaxed the testimonies favoring Gentile inclusion, by pointing out, "The words of the prophets are in agreement with this . . . 'the remnant of men may seek the Lord, and all the Gentiles who bear my name'" (15:15,17).

Luke ends the fourth section, like the previous ones, with a good report of the missionary struggle: "So the churches were strengthened in the faith and grew daily in numbers" (16:5). He is not one to paint a false picture of the easy road laid out for emissaries of the cross. There is hardship and opposition all the way, as there will be wherever the gospel goes. But, when the final report comes in, there will be rejoicing that the battle has been won.

The Gospel Goes to Europe and Asia (16:6-19:20)

The life of Paul as a Christian already has touched Syria, Arabia and Cilicia before what we call his missionary journeys. As I look at a map of the Roman world in that day, and view where Paul establishes churches, I believe I see the plan in his mind. It looks to me that from Antioch of Syria his intention is to plant the gospel seed one Roman province after another in westerly order until they all have been reached.

Once accomplishing church planting in Galatia, the next move would be Asia (our Turkey), then Macedonia and Achaia, followed by Italy and Spain. While that appears to be the strategy, his effort after the province of Galatia is next to approach Asia. This tactic is divinely interrupted. Our missionary record-keeper tells of the workers being "kept by the Holy Spirit from preaching the word in the province of Asia" (16:6). By means of "a vision of a man of Macedonia standing and begging him, 'Come over to Macedonia and help us,'" Paul concludes that God has called for the gospel to be preached in Europe for the first time (16:9-10).

Since Luke writes "*we* got ready" and God "called *us*," the plural pronouns let us know that the team includes Paul, Silas (15:40), Timothy (16:3) and Luke himself (16:10).

Familiar to you will be the conversions of Lydia and the jailer in this city. This new congregation will reflect the variety of persons attracted to the Christian faith. A traveling female business executive and a keeper in charge of criminals will be among the charter members. Their baptism (16:15,33) joins them together in Christ's unifying body, as surely as the faith of the Governor of Cyprus unites him with Joseph, a Levite from the same island (13:12).

It is written, "The Lord opened [Lydia's] heart" (16:14). He accomplished this, using as a key the word brought by Paul. That same Lord opens the prison gates, leading to the baptism of the jailer "and all his family" (16:33). God also opens the doors of Lydia's house for a gathering place for the church. There Paul and Silas meet "with the brothers and encourage them" (16:40). The reader of the account knows that before prison doors, home doors or heart doors open on a virgin field, the heart of God has been opened toward the population long before. Because of God's heart being opened toward the world, missionaries will be "praying and singing hymns to God" (16:25), even before the other gates open.

History again repeats itself when the laborers go to Thessalonica. Initial success in the synagogue (with "some of the Jews persuaded — and . . . a large number of God-fearing Greeks and not a few prominent women"), leads Jews to jealousy (17:2-5). The next attempt at Berea is better received, for "many of the Jews believed, as did also a number of prominent women" (17:11-12). Even so, it becomes necessary again, and for the same reason, for the preachers to depart. This time the next stop will be Athens.

In this famous Greek city, quotes from the Bible that would take their toll in a Jewish synagogue, are replaced by logical reasoning in the marketplace day by day with Epicurean and Stoic philosophers (17:18). Paul's logic challenges them to consider "The God who made the world and everything in it" and the original human from whom "he made every nation of men, that should inhabit the earth" (17:24,26). He speaks of this Creator hoping "men would seek him and perhaps reach out for him and find him" (17:27) and commands "all people everywhere to repent"

(17:30). This different approach for a different area is not as successful in numerical results as other places, but "a few men became followers of Paul and believed" (17:34).

The extension of the work into Corinth finds the tireless Apostle "every Sabbath . . . trying to persuade Jews and Greeks" (18:4). His exclusive preaching "to the Jews" was met by abuse, so once again Paul decides, "From now on I will go to the Gentiles" (18:5-6). Moving from a synagogue base for his operation to a house base (the house of Titus Justus), the result is stated that Crispus the synagogue ruler and many Corinthians "believed and were baptized" (18:8). By a vision, God lets the missionaries know He has "many people in this city" (18:10).

Moving into Ephesus, the lecture hall of Tyrannus becomes the replacement for meeting space. There Paul holds "discussions daily" for "two years" (19:9-10). Did losing the synagogue as the worship center for evangelism, hamper the growth of this salvation movement? Luke answers, "All the Jews and Greeks who lived in the province of Asia heard the word of the Lord" (19:10). The message "spread widely and grew in power" (19:20).

The Gospel Goes to Rome (19:21-28:3)

Once the saving message of Christ gets to Rome, it will go on to Spain and farther on and on. Luke's book to Theophilus will, however, have fulfilled its purpose, when the banner of Christ is planted in Rome, the capital of the world empire. As this last of the six sections commences, the dream is expressed by Paul: "I must visit Rome also" (19:21).

This "must," driving Paul to the city where he will be beheaded eventually, is an inner compulsion, not an outer drive. To brave the odds and go like a David Livingstone to Africa is not some unwanted burden forced on the proclaimer of Christ. It is the call of the Savior dwelling within his witness. When a missionary to China was warned by the people around him, "You will bury yourself in China," his reply was, "I believe in the resurrection!"

Before Paul gets to Rome, the expressed desire of his heart, he must testify more in Ephesus, Troas, Jerusalem and beyond. No method will be left untried. He will teach both "publicly and from house to house" (20:20). He will reach for "both Jews and Greeks (21:21). He will preach in both Greek and "Aramaic" (21:40; 22:2). He will state his case before governors and kings (24:1; 25:24). He will testify "to the gospel of God's grace" (20:24), "the kingdom" (20:25) and "the whole will of God" (20:27). He will spend time incarcerated in Caesarea and shipwrecked near Malta (23:24; 28:1).

He never ceases to marvel at what "God had done among the Gentiles through his ministry" (21:19) plus "how many thousands of Jews have believed" (21:20). He ever is assured that his mission to Rome will become a reality. God revealed to Paul while still in Jerusalem, "As you have testified about me in Jerusalem, so you must also testify in Rome" (23:11). The Apostle to the Gentiles gets that opportunity to testify to Jews in Rome as he did while in Jerusalem; for, while awaiting trial in that universal city, he is free to invite synagogue leaders to come to "his own rented house" (28:30). The synagogue elders come in "large numbers" and listen to him "from morning till evening" (28:23).

We, who with Paul, are commissioned to reach some part of our world, need to be certain of our call. The mission, to the recipients of our message, is "to open their eyes and turn them from darkness to light, and from the power of Satan to God, so that they may receive forgiveness of sins and a place among those who are sanctified" (26:18).

Those who go into difficult mission fields are "not insane," for their story "is true and reasonable" (26:25). Let no one, under Christ's high calling to help with the world, be "disobedient to the vision from heaven" (26:19). The historian Luke traces missionary progress from Jerusalem to

Rome. Today's historians of the church are writing the further chapters of the Acts of the Missionaries. I hope your name will be written in that modern book of Acts.

PART THREE

The Epistles as
Missionary *Correspondence*

CHAPTER 10

Letters From Paul's First
and Second Missionary Thrusts
Galatians, 1 and 2 Thessalonians

The theme of missionary endeavor in the New Testament Scriptures does not begin with Christ's words in Matthew 28 and conclude with Paul's ministry in Acts 28. Jesus' love and compassion for all persons was grounded in the very nature of God taught in the earlier Ancient Scriptures of Israel and revealed most fully in the Savior's life and teachings before his great commission assignment recorded in the last pages of the Gospels. Likewise, after the missionary records in Acts, covering early church expansion, the missionary emphasis of that church history document is not pushed aside for a different priority as we turn to the Epistles. The Letters in the New Testament arise from missionary needs.

Just what is an Epistle? The wag's attempt at humor falls far short in the definition, "An Epistle is the wife of an Apostle." Rather, in fact, the Epistles in our New Testament are written correspondence that substitute for the actual presence of the missionary. Face-to-face conversation by the missionary with a newly formed congregation or a fellow worker would be desirable; but, when geographical space separates, written words on parchment or vellum will be the acceptable substitute.

Out of the white-heat of missionary expansion have come the Letters we now want to consider. There will be no "Epistles from the Twelve to the Jewish church in Jerusalem," for while the apostolic band dwells in that city they can talk with the members orally. It is only after the congregation is disbursed by persecution that it will be necessary for James to write to them as "The twelve tribes scattered among the nations" (James 1:1). So it is that only after Paul leaves an area where he has established a congregation in formerly virgin territory that he will write back to them in order to promote the Christian cause from a distance.

When J.B. Phillips became ready to publish his personal translation of the New Testament Epistles, he followed the suggestion of C.S. Lewis and titled the work *Letters to Young Churches*. That is what those newly-founded congregations were — "Young Churches," recently established by the passionate missionary Paul. Donald Guthrie, commenting on the Pauline Epistles, stresses, "It cannot be too strongly emphasized that the writer of these priceless Christian letters is no arm-chair theologian but a missionary-hearted apostle who encountered and survived more than his fair share of the punishing rigours of life."[1]

The point to be made is that those Letters or Epistles, which have found their way into our New Covenant Scriptures, each relate to missions in a very real way. The penmen fall under the definition of missionaries. The recipients are either newly-founded congregations on the fields where the gospel has gone recently, or they are co-workers of the church planter.

Whether a Letter calls for attention to doctrinal correctness or moral purity, the motivation is to protect the church's witness on the field, lest prospective believers be turned aside. Immoral living belies the Christian testimony that life is transformed by the Savior. Heretical teachings turn minds, from the simple gospel message that saves, to human philosophies that eliminate the Christ of the cross.

---

[1]Donald Guthrie, *The Pauline Epistles: New Testament Introduction* (Chicago: InterVarsity Press, 1961).

As Walter Elliott wrote, "To practical people like Americans there is no oral or written evidence of the true religion so valid as the spectacle of its power to change bad men into good men." He further added, "Such a people will not accept arguments from history and from Scripture, but those of a moral kind they demand, they must see the theories at work."

The Epistles highlight the importance of moral transformation in winning others. They call for harmony in the congregations, lest the world not see what a moral force and unifying power Christ's story is. These Letters appeal for Christ-centered teaching which draw people to the Lord and warn against side issues that drive persons away from him.

As much as we can argue for preferring face-to-face encounters to the substitution of Letters written in one's absence, the circumstance of geographical absence of the missionary from the field has worked for our good. Much, of what long ago was spoken orally, has been lost to us. Some of what had been written is in a form easily duplicated and preserved. In that sense, the Biblical Letters we have are like modern taped lectures. Cassettes can be played and replayed — copied and sent out to others.

Archibald McLean, a prominent missionary leader in early days of the Restoration Movement of the Nineteenth Century, penned the book, *Where the Book Speaks: Mission Studies in the Bible*. He correctly sees the unifying concept, tying together the New Testament in all its parts, as missions. He observed, "What the vertebral column is to the human body, the missionary idea is to the New Testament. . . . If you were to cut missions out of the New Testament it would bleed to death."[2]

---

[2]Archibald McLean, *Where the Book Speaks*, p. 18.

Galatians

At the end of the preaching tour of Paul and Barnabas, that we generally refer to as Paul's first missionary journey, these heralds of the faith return to Antioch of Syria from whence they were commissioned. Not much time passes until they hear that their newly-founded congregations are being upset. Self-sent emissaries from Jerusalem have come to Antioch, Iconium, Lystra and Derbe, informing the Gentile believers that their faith in Christ and subsequent baptism were insufficient to bring them salvation. What was further required of them would be to submit to circumcision and begin keeping the Law of Moses. In other words, every Gentile, to obtain salvation, must first become a Jew in practice.

As soon as this disturbing news reaches the ears of Paul, he fires off this Letter called The Epistle of Paul to the Galatians. "Galatians" is a term that could refer to a people from the Gallic race that had migrated in B.C. times into northern and central Asia Minor. I, rather, take it to have reference to the Roman province by that name, where were the cities referred to in Acts 14. If that is the case, the recipients termed "the churches in Galatia" (1:2) would be Antioch, Iconium, Lystra and Derbe and the time would be A.D. 49, prior to the Jerusalem Conference of Acts 15. Had the Letter been later it is difficult to see why Paul would not have mentioned that important gathering which held to the same conclusion as this Epistle. It is equally hard to understand why the name of Barnabas, mentioned prominently in the second chapter, would be featured for different recipients than those in the above named cities, since he was only Paul's co-worker on this one mission into South Galatia. Add to this the fact that the Letter does not seem to be written several months or years after the founding of these congregations, for what astonishes the Apostle is, he writes, "that you are so quickly deserting the one who called you by the grace of Christ . . . to a different gospel" (1:6).

112

This short letter of six chapters contains Paul's defense of his apostleship (1-2) and of his gospel (3-6). The Judaizing critics were quick to point out that Paul was not included in the original apostolic band of twelve, so Paul gives two chapters to establish his divine call to apostleship. He affirms that he is "an apostle — sent not from men nor by man, but by Jesus Christ" (1:1). He states it was God's pleasure "to reveal his Son in me so that I might preach him among the Gentiles" (1:16; 2:2,7-8). The remaining chapters divide rather evenly into two sections. Chapters 3 and 4 (oversimplified) argue that no Gentile, having accepted Jesus, needs to also become a Jew. Chapters 5 and 6 (at heart) also reason that such a converted Gentile dare not remain a pagan in practice.

This same verdict will come from the Jerusalem Conference. Compare the Conference's conclusion, as given in Acts 15:19-20, with Paul's teaching here. Verse 19 of Acts 15 says, "we should not make it difficult for the Gentiles who are turning to God." Chapters 3 and 4 of Galatians will argue at length to the same decision that these former pagans should not be burdened with law-keeping. Verse 20 in Acts calls for abstinence from the prevalent pagan practices of idolatry, sexual immorality and murder. Chapters 5 and 6 in this Epistle will call for the holiness essential to Christian living.

The Galatian Letter can be called the Roman Epistle in miniature, for both teach salvation is by grace through faith. The believer is free from Jewish law. This freedom in Christ is liberty, but not license. Christians are free from condemnation, but they are not free to sin. Rather, they are free to love God and serve men. They are free, but their freedom is a responsible freedom.

It is correct to call this Letter the Magna Charta of Christian Freedom. But we must understand that, our voluntary submission (enslavement) to Jesus as Lord, is what makes us free from the condemnation awaiting all those under the Law that came through Moses.

One of Paul's illustrations of the purpose of the Mosaic law was to compare it to a tutor. If a pedagogue in Israel prepared a child or youth for future studying at the feet of some Gamaliel in Jerusalem, that teacher's mission ended when the pupil had been handed over to the master teacher. Paul's reasoning is that the Law, like the pedagogue, was to bring its students to Jesus the Master Teacher. At that point the Law's purpose had been accomplished.

In saying, "We are no longer under the supervision of the law" (3:24), the Apostle to the Gentiles is telling these non-Jews who have come to faith and baptism, "You are Abraham's seed, and heirs according to the promise" (3:26-29). Applying another Old Testament story, Paul rejects out-of-hand the Judaizers' teaching by the words, "Get rid of the slave woman and her son" (5:30). His point is that a New Testament Christian is not bound to Old Covenant regulations, for he has identified Hagar as type of the "covenant from Mount Sinai and bears children who are to be slaves" (4:24). Abraham, long before there was that law given through Moses and prior to his being circumcised, was accepted by God because of his faith. The Old Testament record of God's promise to Abraham was, "All nations will be blessed through you" (3:8). That same Old Covenant "Scripture declares that the whole world is a prisoner of sin" (3:22) and in need of the universal gospel.

Why are scholars quick to point to the tone of anger, or the impatience in sound, found in this Letter? The very gospel is at stake. The future of the mission is being compromised. We either save ourselves by our perfect works of law keeping (and that cannot be done), or we are given undeserved forgiveness by the grace of God when we accept Jesus as God's gift to us. Every cult today, with its substitute gospel to replace the real thing, is "zealous to win you over . . . to alienate you from" the apostolic faith (4:17).

Should it be feared that justification by faith in Jesus rather than by works of the law would lead to antinomianism,

Paul uplifts the fruit produced supernaturally by all who are given Christ's Spirit (5:16-26). The call is to "live by the Spirit" and "keep in step with the Spirit" (5:25). The encouragement is to "not become weary" and to "not give up" (6:9).

1 Thessalonians

A young man asked his mentor, "What shall I do for Christ?" The astute answer was, "Go where he is not, and take him with you." Paul's commission must have been understood in much the same way. He has gone to the cities of Cyprus and Galatia where Jesus was not previously known. His present plan is to take the Lord to the cities of Macedonia (Philippi, Thessalonica and Berea) and those of Achaia (Athens and Corinth). It is while at Corinth that Timothy, "God's fellow worker in spreading the gospel of Christ" (3:2), brings an up-to-date report on the Thessalonian congregation. Paul is encouraged to learn they are "standing firm in the Lord" (3:8). His one desire, he says to them, is to "supply what is lacking in your faith" (3:10).

The preaching team's initial effort in the area was forced by a riot to leave after a few short weeks (Acts 17:1-9). Nevertheless, since Thessalonica was the capital of Macedonia, an important seaport and a very large city, it was high on the Apostle's priority list as an area where the gospel banner needed to be planted. Lest opposition come, Paul had learned to travel light. Once the work had been established, Paul could leave and a written message or two could be the replacement for his presence.

The first half of Paul's first Letter to the Thessalonian Christians is filled with the pleasant memory of their initial response to his gospel: "You welcomed the message with the joy given by the Holy Spirit" (1:6). That expression of gladness was increased by the further recollection that the evangelized quickly became evangelists as well. He brought to

115

mind this outcome, writing, "The Lord's message rang out from you not only in Macedonia and Achaia" and became "known everywhere" (1:8). In spite of the physical and mental stress the labor in this major city brought, the result was worth it to the missionaries. They could report how they "turned to God from idols to serve the living and true God" (1:9). Such a visit to that foreign land "was not a failure" (2:1). It took daring "to tell . . . his gospel in spite of strong opposition" (2:2). It took effort to work "night and day in order not to be a burden to anyone" (2:9), but the reward was in the welcome response. In spite of Jewish hostility to keep Paul from "speaking to the Gentiles so that they may be saved" (2:16), the populace "received the word of God . . . not as the word of men, but as it actually is, the word of God" (2:13).

The appeal to the believers in such a hostile environment is "to live lives worthy of God, who calls you into his kingdom and glory" (2:12). The encouragement to the writer is the foreknowledge that kept hardship and trial from being a surprise. The missionary recalls, "In fact, when we were with you, we kept telling you that we would be persecuted. And it turned out that way" (3:4).

The latter portion of the Epistle admonishes continual improvement in lifestyle (4:1-2), constant resistance to the sexual immorality of their heathen environment (4:3-8) and increasing evidence of brotherly love (4:9-10). Do not let the missionary purpose behind each of these moral appeals pass by without notice. Why the plea for the Lord to "make your love increase and overflow for each other and for everyone else" (3:12)? Why the challenge, "Make it your ambition to lead a quiet life, to mind your own business and to work with your hands" (4:11)? Underscore the missionary's answer: "So that your daily life may win the respect of outsiders" (4:12).

"Outsiders" are Paul's target. "Outsiders" are the church's reason for being. God's mission to every congregation is to exist for the winning of "outsiders," so that they become insiders. Is there a zeal in a new convert to win another? "Do not put out the Spirit's fire" (5:19). Even the corrective information on the Second Coming of Christ, letting them know that no deceased believer will miss out on the joys of that day (4:13-5:11), was to keep that worry and concern from diverting the attention of the saved from their ministry toward the lost.

2 Thessalonians

This second Letter to the same people in Thessalonica was written from the same place (Corinth) and possibly in the same year (A.D. 50). A major topic in both Epistles is the Second Coming of the Lord. Where the earlier Letter stresses the certainty of Christ's return, the later Epistle clarifies that "certainty" does not imply "immediacy." An oral report had informed Paul that some were even not doing work, but sitting around idly, waiting for Jesus to come back (3:11).

Such a situation was not to be tolerated. Possibly within a few months after the first Letter, this second one follows denying any truth to some claimed prophecy or purported letter as from Paul affirming Jesus' immediate return (2:1-12). Again, idleness, date-setting and perverted excitement might turn the church, from its difficult but essential mission, to the self-amusement that leads to death. Let each follower of Christ "stand firm and hold to the teachings . . . passed on . . . whether by word of mouth or by letter" from the Apostles (2:15).

The all-consuming desire of obedient subjects of the King of kings is "that the message of the Lord may spread rapidly and be honored" (3:1). The all-inclusive prayer of the Lord's church is "that the name of the Lord Jesus may be glorified" (1:12). The all-compelling hope is that each "will be counted worthy of the kingdom of God, for which" the believers "are suffering" (1:5). Let us never cease to target "Those who do not know God and do not obey the gospel of our Lord Jesus" (1:8). Let us never cease to remember that God calls "Through our gospel, that . . . [persons] might share in the glory of our Lord Jesus Christ" (2:14).

"We constantly pray for you" (1:11) is the explanation why Paul was the successful soul-winner he was. It is difficult to find a Letter from this Missionary of missionaries that is not saturated with prayer. It is impossible to find a better reason for his winning record in Christ's mission from the day of his call on the road to Damascus to his beheading outside the walls of Rome. There may be some question as to who "The man of lawlessness" is, who will set "himself up in God's temple, proclaiming himself to be God" (2:3-4). But there is little doubt who the man of prayer is, who encourages all his congregations to proclaim Jesus as Lord.

Letters From Paul's
Third Missionary Thrust
1 and 2 Corinthians, Romans

Missionary outreach to the whole world can be traced to the Gentile city of Antioch of Syria where Paul and Barnabas were commissioned by the congregation westward to Cyprus and Galatia. Or, it can be followed to its earlier source in Jesus' orders for his followers to disciple the nations. Its earliest origin, in fact, is the heartbeat of God that has so loved the world that Jesus' leaving of heaven for earth and sending his disciples to reach every creature, rises from that unlimited well of divine compassion for all humanity.

Paul, consumed by that Christlike quality of seeking the lost, has set out to evangelize every Roman province. With churches established in Galatia and Europe, the next target is to be Asia with Ephesus as the mission base. It is on this third westward thrust that the Apostle to the Gentiles composes three of his letters famous for their important doctrinal impact. Two letters are addressed to the congregation in Corinth and one epistle to the believers in Rome. The importance of these major population centers is only overshadowed by the significance of these major theological writings by the champion of salvation by grace.

1 Corinthians

True to form our missionary, while establishing new congregations on the untouched field of Asia, has not forgotten the young congregations recently established on the prior mission. So, as he had written to the congregations in Galatia after his first journey and to the Thessalonians after his second trip, he writes now from Ephesus to the Corinthian believers he has recently left behind. So, in addition to his endeavor to preach God's message in this virgin territory which centers in Ephesus, he writes to the Corinthian flock he has recently parented.

From Ephesus, this major seaport and crossroad of highways from every direction, the Apostle writes to the urban center named Corinth, which is located on the narrow strip of land that connects northern Greece with the Peloponnesus, thus making that city the control center of north and south commerce.

The year is thought to be A.D. 55. The letter from Paul is in response to letters from the church seeking answers (7:1,25; 8:4; 12:1; 16:1) and in response to rumors from people (1:10-6:20) that the new work was beset by a host of serious problems, such as factionalism, incest, lawsuits and a long list of other evils.

If your goal is to establish a model society of transformed lives in the midst of pagan surroundings in order to demonstrate the power of the gospel message, you have laid the base for advancing the Christian kingdom. If, however, that demonstration of redeeming power is belied by the practices of some of the so-called "saved," then the experiment will be viewed by the populace as a failure. Paul knows that the success or lack of success in the mission is at stake. His letter aims at rescuing the work of Christ in this pivotal place.

The theme of 1 Corinthians has been worded, "the duty of God's people to live righteous lives." The call for holiness has for its foundation the missionary enterprise. For behavior to be divorced from belief is the pagan way. For life to be transformed by one's convictions regarding Christ is the Christian way. A life turned over to Jesus, body and soul, is so different from what it was, that the world will take notice and consider the cause of such a transformation.

Paul can list the worst of pagan practices, such as adultery, homosexuality, swindling and the like, proudly announcing in the *past* tense, "And that is what some of you were" (6:11). Such life-change is the kind of evidence that will win listeners anywhere in the world. Does the story of Jesus bring genuine conversion, even in a city known for its sexual indiscretion? Does one find the testimony of Christ raised from the dead incredible? Recognize that it is no more unbelievable than a Corinthian living now a holy life! The Greeks, themselves, had coined a word from the city's name (*korinthiazesthai*), meaning to behave as a Corinthian, or to live a debauched life. The Apostle hoped the new name Christian would clearly define the unique lifestyle modeled by Jesus. Our general moral climate in today's western world calls our generation to a careful rereading of Paul's epistle to that day's Corinthians.

Through Ezekiel of old God spoke to the people of Israel about their profaning his name among the nations. The Lord had said, "I will show the holiness of my great name . . . the name you have profaned among them. Then the nations will know that I am the LORD . . . when I show myself holy through you before their eyes" (Ezek. 36:23). Paul is well aware that it is still "through you" — God's people — that God's holiness and grace become visible. As God's spokesman, Paul could say without embarrassment, "my way of life . . . agrees with what I teach everywhere in every church" (4:17).

The call for unity and harmony, rather than division (Chapters 1-4), is also because the decimation that comes from division will disgrace the good news that men from every type of background can find oneness in the Savior.

While immorality is to be expected "outside the church" (5:12), it is not to be tolerated inside (Chapter 5). Otherwise, how will the difference Christ can make in a life be evident? Lawsuits among believers "in front of unbelievers!" is just what it would take to close down the entire Christian mission. Paul, in the light of the church's purpose to win the lost, anguishes, "Why not rather be wronged? Why not rather be cheated?" (6:6). Even when the topic of marital relations between a new Christian and the unconverted husband or wife becomes the theme (Chapter 7), the answer hinges on the soul-winning outcome. "How do you know wife, whether you will save your husband? Or, how do you know, husband, whether you will save your wife" (7:16)? These are questions to be asked. The children's future in or out of Christ is also to determine the action taken, "otherwise your children would be unclean, but as it is, they are holy" (7:14).

Other problems like the freedom to eat food sacrificed to idols (Chapter 8), or paying Christian preachers (Chapter 9), or propriety in public worship (Chapters 10-11), or the misusing of spiritual gifts (Chapters 12-14), etc., also are addressed in a way that considers the success of the mission as top priority.

Read the lines, "We put up with anything rather than hinder the gospel of Christ" (9:12) or, "Do not cause anyone to stumble . . . even as I try to please everybody in every way . . . so that they may be saved" (10:32-33). By such sentences you know that what really counts to the author is the fulfillment of the commission. Why all the instructions on the proper use of the tongues gift? The concern is that "unless you speak intelligible words with your tongue, how will anyone know what you are saying?" (14:9). If "some unbelievers come in, will they not say that you are out of your mind?" (14:23). All practices are to be fine-tuned in order to reach the unbeliever, so that "he will be convinced . . . he is a sinner . . . [and] fall down and worship God" (14:24-25). It matters that the gospel of Christ crucified and risen be preached (Chapter 15) and that generous giving support the proclaimers (Chapter 16) for "a great door for effective work has been opened" (16:9). Let all submit "to everyone who joins in the work and labors at it" (16:16). When it comes to evangelism, Paul's highest advice is, "Follow my example, as I follow the example of Christ" (11:1) and "Always give yourself fully to the work of the Lord" (15:58). The last portion of the letter reveals Paul's next missionary plans.

2 Corinthians

That 2 Corinthians also rightly falls under the designation missionary correspondence is evident throughout, as its author glories in his "ministry that brings righteousness" (3:9) and is succeeding in "reaching more and more people" (4:15). He expresses his hope that his "area of activity . . . will greatly expand" and he "can preach the gospel in the regions beyond" (10:15-16). He gives his job description as "the ministry of reconciliation . . . God reconciling the world to himself in Christ" (5:18-19).

While the mission interest in this Epistle is the same as in the first letter, the changed conditions of the church by A.D. 56 forces Paul to write a defense of his apostleship. He is on one of his confirmation tours that has taken him to Macedonia, from whence he writes this correspondence. Judaizers, claiming to be apostles and carrying letters of recommendation, were undermining Paul's authority; so, in this exceptionally personal letter, Paul defends his ministry.

On these pages we see the missionary undergoing the hardship and suffering that goes with the job to the point of having "despaired even of life" (1:8); but, the distress is carried for the people's "comfort and salvation" (1:6). We see the gospel worker living on the help that comes "in answer to the prayers of many" supporters (1:11) and the encouragement that flows when they "send" the workers on their way

(1:16). We read of "tears" and "the depth" of the gospel-teller's love (2:4). We hear of open doors (2:12) and inner questioning, "Who is equal to such a task?" (2:16). We learn of the "competence [that] comes from God" (3:5) and of not losing heart (4:1).

The Epistle's three parts are: first, Paul's ministry explained (Chapters 1-7); secondly, the offering encouraged (Chapters 8-9); and finally, the congregation warned (Chapters 10-13). At the central section of 2 Corinthians the offering from Gentile believers for poor Jerusalem will cement together these saints into one united body. In the awareness of some hirelings lining their pockets with personal wealth in the name of religion, it is refreshing to see a genuine model who does "not peddle the word of God for profit" (2:17) and does "not use deception, nor . . . distort the word of God" (4:2) as do some while they are preaching themselves rather than Jesus (4:5). Paul's one "goal [is] to please" God (5:9). His one drive is "Christ's love" (5:14). His one support group is "God's fellow workers" (6:1). His one hope is that his "ministry . . . will not be discredited" (6:3).

Even in these central chapters, regarding the offering from Gentile believers to show their kinship with poor Jewish saints, Paul, for missionary reasons, wants "to avoid any criticism . . . taking pains to do what is right . . . in the eyes of men" (8:20-21). The desire to help the needy, coupled with the longing to unify Jewish and Gentile Christians, results in men praising God "for the obedience that accompanies . . . [the] confession of the gospel of Christ" (9:13). Christians are willing to go in purse as well as in person, for the orders of our King reach first our ears, then our hearts and finally our wills, wallets and walk.

The weapons wielded by God's workers are not those "of the world" (10:4). The field assigned by the divine commander brings Paul and Silas to Corinth "with the gospel of Christ" (10:14). The unquenchable search for souls makes these warriors pray that their "area of activity' will "greatly expand . . . [to] regions beyond" (10:15).

Hard work, frequent imprisonments, severe floggings, shipwreck, hunger and cold (11:23-29) is the expected price for a missionary to pay. Why the willingness? Paul's answer is, "What I want is not your possessions but you" (12:14). The test for missionary recruits is difficult. The longing is "that you will discover that we have not failed the test" (13:6).

Romans

On this confirmation tour that has taken Paul from Ephesus through Macedonia, we now find the church planter and church encourager again in Achaia at the city of Corinth. While here, during a three month stay (Acts 20:1-3), he produces the most profound theological work in the New Testament. The year is A.D. 56.

Most of Paul's other church letters are to congregations he has founded and are addressed to particular situations or problems. In this case there are already Christians in Rome, but this apostle to the Gentile world wants them to have record of the gospel he preaches. Since Rome is the largest and most important city in that century, boasting a population between two to four million, it seems essential to Paul that there be a correct understanding of the Christian religion there.

The theme of Romans is that "the gospel . . . is the power of God for the salvation of everyone who believes: first for the Jew, then for the Gentile" (1:16). The book makes clear that acceptability before God is a gift unearned and unearnable. The gift of justification is from God's grace alone and given to any and all upon their putting trust (faith) in God's Son and our Savior. The work from beginning to end is a thoughtful explanation of God's love toward all and the hoped for response that would bring.

The thread of argument is in four parts. Chapters 1-3

establish the lostness in sin of all mankind. The pagan world is lost (Chapter 1). Dialogue with other religions is not on Paul's agenda. Conversion from such religions to Christ is the only way he knows. The Jewish world is also lost (Chapter 2), for having God's law and keeping it are not the same. Paul inquires of the covenant people, "You who brag about the law, do you dishonor God by breaking the law? . . . God's name is blasphemed among the Gentiles because of you" (2:23-24). This means, that if Gentiles are lost and Jews are lost, everyone on earth is in need of the gospel story (Chapter 3). Such irrefutable logic leaves "every mouth . . . silenced and the whole world held accountable to God" (3:19). Missionary work is needed everywhere on earth by every human of all nationalities and religions, since "Jews and Gentiles alike are all under sin" (3:9). The admitted scandal of Christianity is its claim to having the one and only answer to the world's sin problem.

The second portion of the Roman letter moves from the bad news that all "in sin" are lost to the good news that all "in Christ" will be saved (Chapters 4-8). The salvation is by faith and neither by the law nor circumcision. This fact is evidenced by Abraham's acceptance by God prior to his circumcision and years before God's law came through Moses (Chapter 4). God's salvation in Christ is from death (Chapter 5), from sin (Chapter 6), from law (Chapter 7) and from condemnation (Chapter 8). Since God "did not spare his own Son, but gave him up for us all" (8:32), Christ is the Father's solution for the sin disorder that has affected all mankind. We can never have enough knowledge from Greek philosophers, or sufficient good deeds in obedience to divine laws, to make us worthy before God. But, do not despair. God specializes in saving sinners. There is nothing to earn. There is only God's gift to accept. The gift is Christ.

The third section of the epistle wrestles with a logical dilemma that will not just go away. If Jesus is the consummation of all the hopes for a Savior created by the Old

Testament Scriptures (written and preserved by Israel), why have so many Jews not accepted Jesus as their Messiah (Chapter 9-11)? Paul responds as a Christian Jew, showing that this apparent rejection is neither total (Chapter 9), arbitrary (Chapter 10) nor final (Chapter 11).

Listen to the missionary pulse-beat in some of the lines of this section of Paul's treatise. Gentile inclusion is sounded in the phrase "God over all" (9:5) or the prophecy, "I will call them 'my people' who are not my people . . . in the very place where it was said to them 'You are not my people,' they will be called 'sons of the living God'" (9:25-26). Jewish conversion is both the Apostle's prayer, "Brothers, my heart's desire and prayer to God for the Israelites is that they may be saved" (10:1); and the Apostle's hope that "all Israel will be saved" (11:26) in the same manner as the Gentiles by faith.

The clearest step-by-step description of how the lost are to be saved is the unit on salvation for any person confessing Jesus as Lord. Paul rejoices that "everyone who calls on the name of the Lord will be saved," and then asks the insightful questions, "How, then can they call on the one they have not believed in? And how can they believe in the one of whom they have not heard? And how can they hear without one preaching to them? And how can they preach unless they are sent?" (10:13-15). The bottom line is that when the churches send preachers "into all the earth" with their "words [going] to the ends of the earth" (10:18), then Christ's will shall be fulfilled.

The final chapters of the book of Romans (12-16) demonstrate the new life lived by those who take Jesus as Lord. If the earlier chapters show the doctrinal roots of reconciliation, these concluding ones reveal the sanctified fruits of redemption. A holy life manifests love toward fellow believers (Chapter 12), fellow humans (Chapter 13) and the weak of earth (Chapter 14). Chapter 15 quotes Old Testament passages foretelling Gentile inclusion. We read, "I will praise you among the Gentiles" (15:9) from one of the historical books (2 Sam. 22:50); "Rejoice, O Gentiles, with his people" (15:10) from a book of the Law (Deut. 32:43); "Praise the Lord, all you Gentiles, and sing praises to him all you peoples" (15:11) from a Psalm (Ps. 117:1); and "The root of Jesse . . . will arise to rule over the nations; the Gentiles will hope in him" from the Prophets (Isa. 11:10). All parts of the Old Covenant Writings (Law, History, Psalms, Prophets) agree that Gentiles, as well as Jews, are in God's redemption plans.

It is in this fifteenth chapter of Romans that Paul restates his missionary call. He speaks of God's gracious invitation to him "to be a minister of Christ Jesus to the Gentiles with the priestly duty of proclaiming the gospel of God, so that the Gentiles might become an offering acceptable to God" (15:16). He understands that the fruit of his labor is "what Christ has accomplished . . . leading the Gentiles to obey God by what he had "said and done." He reviews what labors he has had "from Jerusalem all the way around to Illyricum" (15:19) and announces his continuing "ambition to preach the gospel where Christ was not known" (15:20).

As Paul looks back on his missionary work in the eastern half of the Mediterranean world as completed, to the degree that his converts can carry the work on; he now looks at Rome as the base for his future work in the western region. "I go to Spain," he writes, adding, "I hope to visit you while passing through and to have you assist me on my journey there" (15:24).

The final chapter lists many names of "fellow workers in Christ" (16:3,9) who "work hard in the Lord" (16:12) at the task of world evangelism. What once was an unknown "mystery hidden for long ages past," is now "made known . . . by the command of the eternal God" (16:25-26). Paul's reference is to Jesus' commission to disciple the nations, so he underscores the church's mission "that all nations might believe and obey him." Thus, the doctrinal work called Romans ends on the mission theme with which it began. Paul sees his apostleship as the order to "call people from among all the Gentiles to the obedience that comes from faith" (1:5). Each previous and present plan of Paul to come to Rome was to "have a harvest . . . just as . . . among the other Gentiles" (1:13). To that task he is "obligated" (1:14), "eager" (1:15) and "not ashamed" (1:16).

CHAPTER 12

Letters from Paul's
Fourth Missionary Thrust
Colossians, Philemon, Ephesians, Philippians

The book of Acts closed with Paul in Rome awaiting trial. Luke ended his account with the good news that the Apostle was allowed to reside "in his own rented house" and during the two years (A.D. 61-63) was allowed to tell Christ's story to all who came to see him. The last line by Luke was, "Boldly and without hindrance he preached the kingdom of God and taught about the Lord Jesus Christ" (Acts 28:31). What Luke did not write was the further good news that Paul could write letters of encouragement to Christian churches and believing friends.

Of the letters he wrote during this time we have four. Three of these were written at about the same time — some suggest on the very same day. The other was penned later, reflected by the optimism of an anticipated soon release. Colossians, Philemon and Ephesians we date around A.D. 61 and Philippians 62.

Each letter shows pastoral concern for the newly founded congregations and gives helpful advice to members who share the burden of continuing the mission. Our naming Colossians first in the listing will be explained in a moment. Now, let us again be reminded that the present order of the twenty-seven books in our New Testament is not to be explained on the basis of chronology.

Colossians and Philemon

When Paul was bringing his testimony to Christ on the third missionary journey to the Roman Province of Asia, you remember the base for that outreach was to be Ephesus. Others on his team were to take the gospel story 100 miles east to Colossae. Although the new converts at this mission outpost had not met Paul "personally" (2:1), they had, through Epaphras, been informed of his state.

The scenario appears to be something like this. A new heresy, distorting the gospel at its core, has spread into the Lycus valley and threatens the new work. Epaphras, the preacher, does not perceive how to handle the error, but knows Paul will know what to do. So, out of loving concern for this flock of Christ's sheep, he sets out for Rome to find the Apostle who can save the day.

Upon reporting to the Apostle the nature of this error, that teaches that only the elite have the key to secret knowledge, Paul takes pen in hand and writes this Christ-exalting letter in refutation of this "incipient Gnosticism" that degrades Jesus and erects a class system. The Colossian congregation is meeting in the home of Philemon, so it is appropriate that one letter should be written to the congregation and another personal note to the host.

The second of the letters is especially fitting, for in the Roman prison has been a runaway slave, Onesimus, who has fled far away to Rome from his master Philemon. Paul's co-worker Tychicus can return the now converted Onesimus and deliver the letter for the church and add oral amplification at the same time (4:7-9). Obviously no boat from Rome can dock inland at Colossae, but will more likely land at Ephesus. This makes it probable that a letter similar to the Colossian Epistle will be dropped off on the way at the Ephesian church by the same letter-bearer, Tychicus. The many similarities between the Colossian and Ephesian letters are so apparent they cannot be missed. Colossians is more specific and Ephesians more general, leading some to surmise that Paul made more than one copy of the epistle we call Ephesians, leaving it to Tychicus to write in "to the saints in Ephesus" (Eph. 1:1) or "Laodicea" (Col. 4:16) or wherever else he visited on the way.

I find it helpful to name the emphasis of Colossians as "The Glorious Christ of the Church" and of Ephesians "The Glorious Church of the Christ." Either title suggests we need not seek salvation from another. Christ is all-sufficient. We need not leave the Lord's church for some other group. Asian mysticism (2:18-19), Greek philosophy (2:8-9), Jewish legalism (2:10-17), or Ascetic regulations (2:20-23) have nothing to offer the church. There are no deficiencies in Christ's gospel. Let Colossians know they have a colossal Lord (Chapter 1), a colossal Faith (Chapter 2) and have shared in a colossal Baptism (Chapter 3-4). Let modern Christians rest assured that the religious cults of our time have no truth to offer those in the all-sufficient Christ who is "the way and the truth and the life" (John 14:6). Beware of the theological "tossed salads" being temptingly offered today in the name of broad-mindedness. Christ is all you need! Everyone needs Christ! So everyone needs the missionary's message!!

Regarding God's one saving message of Christ for the whole world, Paul affirms, "We proclaim him, admonishing and teaching everyone with all wisdom, so that we may present everyone perfect in Christ" (1:28). As to the success of the mission, thirty some years after Jesus gave the great commission, Paul can assert, "All over the world this gospel is bearing fruit and growing" (1:6). He can add, "This is the gospel that you heard and that has been proclaimed to every creature under heaven" (1:23).

It thrills Paul to be a part of Christ's glorious church, so he rejoices, "I have become its servant by the commission God gave me to present to you the word of God in its fullness" (1:22). He clearly defines his reason for being, writing, "My purpose is . . . that they may know the mystery of God, namely, Christ" (2:2). He rallies the congregation's participation in the furtherance of the gospel's spread, requesting, "Devote yourselves to prayer . . . that God may open a door for our message, so that we may proclaim the mystery of Christ. . . . Pray that I may proclaim it clearly, as I should" (4:2-4). He further calls for the kind of living before the eyes of the world that will draw them to the gospel's light. "Be wise in the way you act toward outsiders; make the most of every opportunity . . . know how to answer everyone" (4:5-6).

In Philemon, the shortest of Paul's letters, we learn that the congregation met in his home (Phlm. 2) and that he was a man of prayer (Phlm. 22). Most important to the soul-winner Paul was this church leader's priority at the same task. Paul's intercession for his co-worker friend is, "I pray that you may be active in sharing your faith" (Phlm. 6).

Ephesians

The book of Revelation makes reference to seven major churches in Asia at the end of the first century. These and many others were outgrowths of Paul's missionary efforts in Ephesus and out from that center. Paul was never hesitant to speak a good word for Christ. He was never one to minimize the significance of the church, as some do today. To the Apostle, the church of Jesus Christ worshipped a glorious God (Chapter 1), experienced a glorious Salvation (Chapter 2), shared in a glorious Ministry (Chapter 3), manifest a glorious Unity (Chapter 4), followed a glorious Walk (Chapter 5) and battled in a glorious Conquest (Chapter 6).

Nothing concerning the church is more glorious than its divinely appointed place in reaching the lost. It is God's "eternal purpose" and "His intent . . . that now, through the church, the manifold wisdom of God should be made known" (3:10-11). "Gentiles by birth" (2:11) and "without hope" (2:12) need to learn that "now in Christ Jesus" the once "far away have been brought near through the blood of Christ" (2:13). They "consequently . . . are no longer foreigners and aliens, but fellow citizens with God's people" (2:19). "It has now been revealed . . . that through the gospel the Gentiles are heirs together with Israel" (3:5-6). Children need to know this "training and instruction" (6:4), as do slaves and masters (6:5-9).

Each Christian, like a soldier girt for battle under Christ's command, should clad himself in full armor and take "the sword of the Spirit, which is the word of God" (6:14-17) and enter the battle for the souls of men. It is for the purpose of carrying out Jesus' "purpose and will" (1:5) that we have been chosen and predestined.

To be "included in Christ when you heard the word of truth, the gospel of your salvation" (1:13), ought to make us glad to be in his church. It ought to make one and all, like Paul, to become "a servant of this gospel" and by God's provided grace "preach to the Gentiles the unsearchable riches of Christ, and to make [this] plain to everyone" (3:7-9). Should any of us feel inadequate at sharing the faith, rely on the Commander behind the commission "who is able to do immeasurably more than all we ask or imagine, according to his power that is at work in us" (3:20). Do not let your timid soul forget God is "over all and through all and in all" (4:6). It is Christ that "prepares God's people for works of service, so that the body of Christ may be built up" (4:12). How will church growth take place? It "grows and builds itself up in love, as each part does its work" (4:16).

To be most effective at the single task of preaching, baptizing and teaching, "be careful . . . how you live . . . making the most of every opportunity" (5:15-16). Paul's prayer should be our daily prayer: "Whenever I open my mouth [may] words . . . be given me so that I will fearlessly make known the mystery of the gospel" (6:19).

Philippians

The Philippian letter is a thank you note to the first Christian congregation in Europe. In its membership would be Lydia and her household and the jailer and his family whose conversions are told in Acts 16. Mentioned in the salutation of the Epistle, in addition to the saints, are "the overseers and deacons" (1:1). Funds under the oversight of the church leaders had reached Paul through Epaphroditus. Special thanks to the eldership for such support will reach the ears of the membership.

Such financial backing in fulfilling the mission is described as "partnership in the gospel from the first day until now" (1:5). Paul recalls those initial times in Philippi, writing, "In the early days of your acquaintance with the gospel, when I set out from Macedonia, not one church shared with me in the matter of giving and receiving, except you only; for even when I was in Thessalonica, you sent me aid again and again when I was in need" (4:15-16).

Like "Johnny One Note," singing the same tune over and over, Paul strikes again and again the one purpose that rings repeatedly in his mind. The imprisonment he suffers is not resented, because what "happened . . . really served to advance the gospel" (1:12) and that is the Apostle's one concern. He rejoices, "It has become clear throughout the whole palace guard and to everyone else that I am in chains for Christ" (1:13). His personal courage to speak out has resulted in "most of the brothers in the Lord" giving out "the word of God more courageously and fearlessly" (1:14).

Paul could not see himself carrying banners on a street corner for some political cause or social-action goal. He would not likely have been described as a worshipper who, by body swaying and voice intonation, was recognized as a specialist in praise. Yet, his focus on soul winning did more to bring justice in society and more voices lifting praise to God in assemblies than having given his life to the substitute routes.

As the model for the ministers needed everywhere and at every time, Paul focuses on evangelism. To him, "the important thing is that in every way . . . Christ is preached" (1:18). That priority brings forth the counsel, "Conduct yourselves in a manner worthy of the gospel of Christ . . . contending as one man for the faith of the gospel" (1:27). The apostolic call to the membership is to be "one in spirit and purpose" (2:2). And what is that purpose to which each believer is to give his time and effort? The unified effort of the believers is to be toward the goal "that at the name of Jesus every knee should bow . . . and every tongue confess that Jesus Christ is Lord" (1:10-11).

The purpose of the church is the purpose of God. That purpose of God has been made known through His Son, as he sought to save the lost. Diversion from God's will happens when "everyone looks out for his own interests, not those of Jesus Christ" (2:21). Christ's interest is people. Timothy, who "has served . . . in the work of the gospel" (2:22), by that ministry has exemplified Christlikeness. Now let all Philippians "shine like stars in the universe as you hold out the word of life" (2:15-16). The call for good news tellers is not alone for the ears of men like Timothy, but also for women like Euodia and Syntyche, who "contended" at Paul's "side for the cause of the gospel" (4:3).

To confess "Jesus is Lord" at one's baptism into Christ is to commit oneself to practicing what Jesus preached and giving oneself to the cause for which he died. To be non-missionary is to be *anti* the cause of Christ. Purpose determines actions. To miss Christ's purpose emphasized in the Gospels, Acts and Epistles leaves a church tossed about in many directions and by many winds of doctrine. The compass of Scripture and the North Star of Apostolic example keep the sincere believers on course.

CHAPTER 13

Letters from Paul's
Final Missionary Thrust
Titus, 1 and 2 Timothy

We come now to the "Twenty-ninth Chapter of Acts." When Luke concluded his record of the Acts of the Apostles at Chapter 28, he had reached his writing goal of tracing the growth of the church from Jerusalem, the capital of Judaism to Rome, the capital of the world. But while he stopped his church growth record at this point, the evangelistic expansion did not come to an end.

Released from prison with charges dropped, Paul, according to early Patristic tradition, continues his missionary thrust westward. The earlier expressed desire in the Roman letter to "go unto Spain" (Rom. 15:24), now finds fulfillment. Clement of Rome tells of the Apostle going to "the extremity of the west" (i.e., Spain).

Yet Paul is not one to rush to a new field without first securing the missionary churches he has already founded. So with his eyes to the west, he leaves the Roman prison to first check on the Christian work in the east. He takes Titus to the isle of Crete (Titus 1:5) to oversee the Lord's cause there and sends Timothy to Ephesus to strengthen the congregations in Asia (1 Tim. 1:3), while he confirms the believers in Macedonia before heading to the virgin field of Spain.

He has given oral instruction already to his co-workers Timothy and Titus, but puts their orders in written form as he writes back to them from Macedonia. Should anyone question these young men's authority as they travel from church to church, the letters 1 Timothy or Titus should clarify their apostolic backing. The date I place on these epistles is A.D. 64.

Since the Eighteenth Century, these letters with 2 Timothy have been called the "Pastoral Epistles." Granted these letters, like all of Paul's, show pastoral concern. But Timothy and Titus are not "pastors" in the Biblical sense of the word. Pastoring, or shepherding, a congregation is the privilege and responsibility of local elders. Paul's sons in the gospel are his delegates to see that proper pastoring is being done in every church across Crete (by Titus) and Asia (by Timothy).

Because missionary orders call for both discipling and teaching the obedience to everything Christ commanded (Matt. 28:19), leaving baptized believers behind is not enough. Missionary work includes strengthening in the faith, as well as bringing to faith.

1 Timothy and Titus

Young Timothy has been with Paul on his missionary endeavors from the second journey unto this point and will remain with him until his martyrdom. This personal and practical letter to him gives its purpose. Paul states, "I am writing you these instructions so that . . . you will know how people ought to conduct themselves in God's household, which is the church of the living God" (3:14-15). Timothy in his congregational visits is to look for the proper behavior of teachers (Chapter 1), of worshippers (Chapter 2), of elders and deacons (Chapter 3) and of evangelists (Chapters 4-6).

The key verses of the letter are 1 Timothy 3:15-16. Concern for the lifestyle, behavior or "conduct" in each church, is because Christ's church is "the pillar and foundation of the truth." The mission of the Christian community is to uphold the gospel. It is to serve as an unshaking foundation for the truth of God.

At this point Paul quotes an early church hymn that succinctly delineates "the truth" the believing community is supporting. In a nutshell this is the great mystery of godliness: "He appeared in a body, was vindicated by the Spirit, was seen by angels, was preached among the nations, was believed on in the world, was taken up in glory." "He appeared in a body" is the gospel story from the incarnation to the cross. "Vindicated by the Spirit" is the resurrection from the grave by the Holy Spirit, showing Christ vindicated, or acquitted, from the charge of blasphemy in his claim of deity. "Seen of angels" is the appearances before the messengers we call the apostles to establish the reality of the resurrection fact. "Preached among the nations" is reference to the apostolic witness of what they had seen of the living Christ to even the Gentile world. "Believed on in the world" is testimony to the success of the gospel story to bring hearers to faith. "Taken up in glory" is reference to the ascension into heaven by Jesus after his forty days of post-resurrection appearances.

Timothy is to see that the congregations of the living Lord not get sidetracked by "myths and endless genealogies" (1:4), which "is falsely called knowledge" (6:20) or *gnosis* (i.e., Gnosticism). Such heresy will "promote controversies rather than God's work" (1:4), which is fulfilling Christ's commission. It is "sound doctrine," when it "conforms to the glorious gospel" (1:10-11). And what is the basic goal of that gospel? The "trustworthy saying . . . Christ Jesus came into the world to save sinners" (1:15).

If saving sinners is the mission, then let prayers "be made for everyone" including "kings and all those in authority," for "God our Savior . . . wants all men to be saved and to come to a knowledge of the truth" (2:1-4). Let every missionary remember that "Jesus Christ . . . gave himself as a ransom for all men" (2:6). Paul will not forget that it was "for this purpose" he was "appointed . . . a teacher of the true faith to the Gentiles" (2:7). Because the church exists not for its members but for the people not yet Christian, it is important that those persons be placed in leadership that "have a good reputation with outsiders" and "be men worthy of respect" (3:7-8). Let "no one . . . be open to blame" (5:7). Let no one "give the enemy . . . opportunity for slander" (5:14). Even let the enslaved act in such a way as believers "that God's name and our teaching . . . not be slandered" (6:1). Let Christian living be practiced, because such silent testimony to the truth of the gospel will not go unheard, in that "good deeds are obvious, and . . . cannot be hidden" (5:25). God's call to every convert is to "fight the good fight of the faith" (6:12) and "guard what has been entrusted to your care" (6:20).

The letter to Titus, carrying the same missionary burden as 1 Timothy, calls on the various groups in the church (elderly, young, enslaved) to so live "that in every way they will make the teaching about God our Savior attractive" (2:9-10). Actions do speak louder than words and they either attract or repel. The Apostle who has given his life bringing God's "word to light through the preaching . . . commanded of God" (1:3), does not want poor example in the people to cloud out effective teaching from the proclaimer. The church must act as a team together, living attractively and preaching effectively. Personal example is the necessary foundation for successful evangelism. Basic also is congregational backing and support. "Do everything you can to help" fellow workers and "see that they have everything they need" (3:13).

2 Timothy

In the Roman persecution of Christians under Nero in A.D. 64 Peter, according to tradition, was crucified upside down. Paul escaped death at that time only because he was in distant Spain, but at the end of that mission he has returned to Rome and is imprisoned as a Christian propagandist. This imprisonment is not like the house arrest and chains of the earlier restraint at which time he wrote the "prison epistles." This time it is solitary confinement and almost certain decapitation.

The final letter by Paul to his son in the faith is very personal and full of promise. The often used words "remember" or "remembrance," coupled with "not ashamed," suggest the content of unashamed memories (Chapter 1), unashamed ministry (Chapter 2), unashamed warnings (Chapter 3) and unashamed charges (Chapter 4). Paul's "Swan Song" or "Last Will and Testament" calls for the continuation of the mission to which he had given his life.

Addressing this final call to the partner in mission whom Paul calls "Timothy, my dear son" (1:2), the Apostle would ask that he "do the work of an evangelist" (4:5). Faith only comes from hearing the story of Christ, so the gospel must be told. Many kind actions might consume the preacher's days and hours, but these good works without the telling of the greatest story ever told will not leave behind believers and Christian congregations.

Timothy for many years was Paul's helper. Now he must become Paul's voice. That being true, Paul calls on his co-worker not to remain but a warm ember. It is time "to fan into flame the gift of God," which had been given Timothy when the Apostle laid hands upon him (1:6). Paul's son in the gospel must overcome his "timidity" and "not be ashamed to testify about our Lord" (1:7-8). The hour has come to "join . . . in suffering for the gospel" (1:8), because it was for "this gospel . . . [Paul was] suffering" (1:11-12).

The young "son" must now become the grown man, ready to "guard the good deposit that was entrusted." This he is fully equipped to do "with the help of the Holy Spirit" (1:14). What has been "entrusted" to him, he must "entrust to reliable men who will also be qualified to teach others" (2:2). If Paul's life can be taken away so can the lives of his co-workers. Since the evangelization of the world is to continue after each present worker is personally stopped by death, the multiplication of workers is the divinely appointed way. Each man with the mission is to recruit converts, but also raise up future workers. The only qualification for these laborers is that such be "reliable" and "qualified." Each congregation is wise to count not only how many ministers have served that body, but how many ministers it has raised up to serve the work across the world.

The last time Paul will express in writing the inner drive that has controlled all his actions, he writes it for all the world to see. His purpose is that "the message might be fully proclaimed and all the Gentiles might hear it" (4:17). He reminds the one who will continue his work, "You . . . know all about . . . my purpose" (3:10). To fulfill that purpose he must do his best to be "a workman . . . who correctly handles the word of truth" (2:15) and will "preach the Word . . . in season and out of season" (4:2). What he will not do is get "involved in civilian affairs [if] he wants to please his commanding officer" (2:4).

The great command of Christ the "commanding officer" focuses the army of believers on its high command of soul-winning. The most demonic but alluring of Satan's devices to get the church off course, is to offer high roads that appear so right that Christian energies and efforts are depleted leaving little time or place for evangelism. Stick to the compass of "God's word" (2:9), the "holy Scriptures" (3:15), which guide men to "obtain the salvation that is in Christ Jesus" (2:10). Major in Scripture and "the man of God . . . [will] be thoroughly equipped" (3:17). Major in minors and the battle for souls is lost.

When Royal J. Dye, missionary of the Christian Church for many years in what was then called the Belgian Congo, was forced by age and health to stop his labors for black Africans, he made it clear that he did not sacrifice when he went to Africa. Rather, his greatest sacrifice was when he had

144

to come home to the United States. So concludes Paul's suffering and hardship for Christ's cause. As he waits for the sound of feet walking to his prison cell to get him for the execution certain to come, he considers being stopped from telling the lost of the world's Savior the greatest sacrifice he has been called upon to make. Yet, when they bound him, "God's word . . . [was] not chained" (2:9) and when they take his life as messenger of the cross, the message will continue to live.

CHAPTER 14

Letters Related to Jewish Evangelism
James, Hebrews

One of the *great* qualities of the *great* commission is its *great* concern for follow up. The "go and make disciples . . . baptizing them" (Matt. 28:19) is only the beginning task for the missionary. The Lord of the church did not put a period at the end of that imperative, fold up his materials, go his way to glory and imply that once a hearer is baptized the work is accomplished.

My momentary joy at reading today of thousands in Russia or India who after hearing a sermon or two, have responded favorably to the gospel, is tempered by the sober realization that the heralds, sometimes after only a week of ministry, have moved on and the "babes in Christ" have been left to make it on their own. The wiser Christ called for the initiatory baptism to be followed by "teaching them to obey everything I have commanded you."

The follow-up is to include more than teaching *some* of Jesus' commands. The newborn believer is to learn "everything" Christ commanded. The task of follow-through is not the work of a month or so, for the mission is not over until the baptized "obey" each instruction. Men like Peter, Paul, James or John can and do move to new fields to plant the gospel seed there, but a congregation must be established where nurture of converts can continue under the supervising eyes of elders qualified to shepherd their entrusted flock.

This brings us to letters like James and Hebrews that especially relate to evangelism of Jews. In both instances persons had been brought to believer's baptism, but now, after much time, some drifting or falling away is beginning to occur. The importance of keeping the sheep in the fold is as basic as winning them to the fold in the first place. Salvation is at stake.

We have been following Paul, the special apostle to the uncircumcised, who wrote letters from his early epistle to the Galatians in A.D. 49 to his last written correspondence in 67. It is time to look at letters to circumcised Jewish believers, the first written in A.D. 49, at about the time of Galatians, and the last at around A.D. 68, shortly after 2 Timothy.

James

The author James is Jesus' half-brother, to whom Christ had made a special appearance following his resurrection (1 Cor. 15:7). With earlier doubts and reservations totally removed, James has become one of the "pillars" (Gal. 2:9) of the first Christian congregation in the world. The converts in Jerusalem, from Pentecost A.D. 30 on, kept growing in number from the original three thousand. The exceptional progress of the gospel was threatened when, at the stoning of Stephen, the church's first martyr, "a great persecution broke out against the church in Jerusalem. All except the apostles were scattered throughout Judea and Samaria" (Acts 8:2). This bad news was not so bad, because "those who had been scattered preached the word wherever they went" (Acts 8:4).

I believe this scattering referred to in Acts 8 is the same dispersion under consideration in the salutation of James 1:1 that reads, "To the twelve tribes scattered among the nations." The congregation had grown in the faith under James' teaching, so that on leaving the city under stress, they went out preaching "wherever they went." But now, after

many years (15?) away from their home base, they have
grown lax and are in need of "teaching, rebuking, correcting
and training in righteousness" (2 Tim. 3:15).

Martin Luther is often quoted in his disappointment that
so little of the gospel facts and promises are stated in this
epistle of five chapters. Luther calls the letter an "epistle of
straw," in light of Paul's comment that on the foundation of
Christ some workers build with "gold, silver, costly stones,
wood, hay or stubble" (1 Cor. 3:12). The sixteenth century
reformer places the Epistle of James in the appendix of his
German translation of the New Testament, showing his
unwillingness to classify it with the rest of the other biblical
documents which lift high Jesus' death and resurrection.

I call your attention to the fact that Paul, who is famous
for restating the gospel in his writings, often is heavy on
doctrine in the first portion of a letter and turns to practical
matters in the latter section. The recipients of James' epistle
have heard sermons from this pastor in Jerusalem over the
years. They are well aware of his testimony regarding the one
he acknowledges as "the Lord Jesus Christ" (1:1; 2:1). His
circular letter to them is like the second part of a Pauline
letter, calling for the lifestyle expected of a follower who has
received the forgiveness from God attributed to Jesus' death
and resurrection. James is the only New Testament book to
mention Old Testament Job. The point of the appeal is "Job's
perseverance" (5:11) to be followed by every disciple of
Christ. Clinging tenaciously to faith in God in spite of trials is
the stick-to-it-ive-ness desired of every believer. Of what value
is an initial faith and baptism that is not followed by enduring faith.

To hear this epistle read is to hear echoes of Jesus'
sermon on the mount. The letter reflects more of Christ's
words than all the other New Testament letters. Some scholars identify twenty-three recollections of Jesus' hillside
message as preserved by Matthew (Chapters 5-7). James' style
of teaching radiates the influence his half-brother had on

him. The work can correctly be titled "Common Sense Christianity."

When you read his document in Greek, you are impressed by the fact that the name James in Greek is Jacob (*Jacobus*). You may call to mind Genesis 49 where the Old Testament Jacob gathers his twelve sons about him and makes a dozen predictions about their future. This has led some to identify twelve topics in the letter of James. What others have termed individual and different gems, strung together on a string to make the beautiful necklace we call this practical letter, is now considered twelve different truths to instruct the New Israel, God's present "twelve tribes."

There are about twelve themes in the epistle and can be studied in these units: (1) Trials and Steadfastness (1:2-12); (2) Evil and Good (1:13-18); (3) Hearing and Doing (1:19-27); (4) Riches and Poverty (2:1-13); (5) Faith and Works (2:14-26); (6) Blessing and Cursing (3:1-12); (7) Harmony and Faction (3:13-18); (8) Self-exaltation and Divine-exaltation (4:1-12); (9) Life and Death (4:13-17); (10) Selfishness and Judgment (5:1-6); (11) Enduring and Quitting (5:7-12) and (12) Sick Bodies and Sick Souls (5:13-20).

The man James was labeled "Camel Knees," because he wore calluses on his knees praying in pastoral concern for his flock. The epistle James is titled, "The Amos of the New Testament," since he shows such concern for justice and mercy. I am willing to call both the man and the book evangelistic because, like Paul and his letters, the appeal for lives consistent with the Christian profession is basic to the ongoing mission. The genuineness of Christianity is known by the life results in its constituents. This missionary concern is indelibly present in the Epistle's closing sentence, "My brothers, if one of you should wander from the truth and someone should bring him back, remember this: Whoever turns a sinner from the error of his way will save him from death and cover over a multitude of sins" (5:19-20).

Hebrews

That the Epistle to the Hebrews is addressed to Hebrew Christians is not established by the title, but rather from the general character of the material that constitutes its thirteen chapters. The words "to the Hebrews" are not a part of the original manuscript, but such a title is attached very early because a Jewish-Christian audience seems clearly implied.

Like James was addressed to "the twelve tribes" (James 1:1) to whom Jesus Christ was Lord in order to hold them steadfastly to the church, so Hebrews is a "word of exhortation" (13:22), or written sermon, to keep Jews who have accepted Jesus as Messiah from apostasizing from the church. The writer sees a spiritual condition, where the persons addressed are about to "drift away" (2:1), "throw away . . . confidence" (10:35) or "grow weary" (12:3). The brothers are to see that not one individual "turns away" (3:12).

The danger of apostasy is threatening (6:4-8; 10:26-29; 12:14-19). The need for renewed zeal is called for (6:9-12; 10:19-39; 12:12-17).

Consider this as the possible life-situation that brought forth this systematic and eloquent defense of New Testament Christianity. The recipients are the Jewish Christians Paul has made when brought to Rome for trial. You remember that Paul, whose calling is to reach Gentiles, is promised by God in Jerusalem at his arrest, "As you have testified about me in Jerusalem (i.e., to Jews), so you must also testify in Rome (i.e., to Jews)" (Acts 23:11). That promise is fulfilled when, to "his own rented house" (Acts 28:30) in Rome, come rabbis from Rome's Jewish synagogues requesting, "we want to hear what your views are" (Acts 28:22). Luke's seemingly equal reporting of outcome as, "some believed . . . and some disbelieved" (Acts 28:24) has led some like R.C.H. Lenski to conclude that half of Rome's thirteen local synagogues may have become Christian synagogues in the Pauline imprisonment years of A.D. 61-63. The closing salutation, "Those from Italy send you their greetings" (13:24) indicates a special attachment between the associates of the author and the recipients. Likely these former residents of Italy's capital city want to greet the ones in that city who have, like themselves, put faith in Christ. As early as A.D. 95, Clement of Rome is evidence of Christians in Rome knowing this epistle and giving the nod of approval.

Since Acts 28, suffering has come upon followers of Christ in the persecutions under Nero (A.D. 64-68). The long-time church in that city, composed of Jews and Gentiles, is paying with hardship and death itself. These synagogues newly influenced toward Christ by Paul, are not as yet known by the oppressing government as churches of Christ but are still considered synagogues of the Jews.

The temptation is real. When recognized as followers of Christianity, then death and pain will be theirs. To drop Christ seems not such a fatal option to them, for Jehovah, the ancient Scriptures and temple can still be theirs. The epistle is thorough refutation of such a possibility. To go back on their baptismal confession would be to trample "the Son of God under foot" and insult "the Spirit of grace" (10:29). If Messianic Jews, to save their necks, will leave Christ and his church, what other sons of Abraham, Isaac and Jacob will be open to his initial call?

With unwavering logic Apollos[1] (or some other author "eloquent . . . and . . . mighty in the scriptures" [Acts 18:24]) upholds the Christian faith as superior to Judaism in Message (Chapters 1-2), Deliverance (Chapters 3-4), Mediation (Chapters 5-7) and Covenant (Chapters 8-10). The appeal is to continuing Faith (Chapter 11), Hope (Chapter 12) and Love (Chapter 13). Once the Jewish temple is destroyed in A.D. 70 under the siege of Titus and temple worship becomes an impossibility, the possibility of returning to Old

---

[1]Hebrews 2:3 seems to list the author as a second generation Christian who received the gospel through apostles and was not one himself.

Testament ways becomes next to impossible. The present-tense verbs used regarding the worship associated with the temple and its priesthood indicate the Epistle is written before the destruction under Rome has occurred (8:4,13; 9:4-5,9; 10:1,8,11; 13:10-11). The key word "superior" (1:4) or "better" is used thirteen times to clarify that moving from Jewish roots to Christ is ascending to higher ground, but leaving Jesus for Old Covenant ways is a downhill choice. The writer says "superior" is the word for Jesus over the law that came through angels (1:4) and "better" is the term for our "things" (6:9), our "priest" (7:7), our "hope" (7:19), our "covenant" (7:23), our "promises" (8:6), our "sacrifices" (9:23), our "possessions" (10:34), our heavenly "country" (11:16), our "resurrection" (11:35), our "plans" (11:40) and our "word" (12:24).[2]

Only Jesus "provided purification for sins" (1:3). World salvation is dependent on Christ. "He suffered death, so that by the grace of God he might taste death for everyone" (2:9). "Everyone" without exception is the job description of those on a mission under Christ's leadership. If "the universe was formed at God's command" (11:3), such a Creator cannot limit his interest to one tribe of earth or one type of human. If this one God is to be in the future "the judge of all men" (12:23), he would desire to be in the present the savior of all. The Old Testament story of salvation history introduces the readers to Abraham, a type of all who will walk by faith. Will the believers who descend in faith from Abraham be few? The situation will be quite otherwise. They will be "as numerous as the stars in the sky and as countless as the sands of the seashore" (11:12).

If such multitudes are to be reached for Christ, and reached by the church God has redeemed, how can such a host of humans be touched in our lifetime? Hear the author's closing prayer: "May the God of peace . . . equip you with

---

[2]The word "better" is used twice in 8:6.

everything good for doing his will, and may he work in us what is pleasing to him" (13:21). "His will" is for "all men to be saved and to come to a knowledge of the truth" (1 Tim. 2:4). "What is pleasing for him?" That "everyone come to repentance" (2 Pet. 3:9). For everyone to come to repentance will demand more Christians to go into the field of labor. It is a matter of come and go. When we go at Christ's command, sinners will come in response to Jesus' invitation.

CHAPTER 15

Letters From Peter, Jude and John
2 Peter, Jude, 1 Peter, 1, 2 and 3 John

Long sermons are not, by that criteria alone, more effective than less extensive ones. Likewise, briefer letters are not less potent for good because they are shorter. Certainly 2 and 3 John or Jude are not to evangelism what the Roman Epistle, the Gospel according to John or the Acts of the Apostles are. Still there are many believers who owe their personal salvation to some caring soul who wrote a short note of encouragement at just the right time, or who penned a morale-building one-page-memo just when it was needed.

The letters in the New Testament we have saved to look at last are often classified as general epistles. However we choose to title them, they prove that God, from the first Christian century, has used personal visits and personal correspondence as a tool in advancing His mission. We will begin this final classification of epistles with a three chapter letter (2 Peter) and a one page tract (Jude). The author of 2 Peter is the former fisherman, whom Christ called to be a fisher of men (Luke 5:10) and saw in that life the potential for solid service and unquaking conviction, nicknaming him "a rock" (Matt. 16:18). The writer of the epistle of Jude is "a brother of James" (verse 1), who in humility like James does not call attention to that human connection with Jesus as half-brother (Mark 6:3), but chooses to refer to himself only as "a servant of Jesus Christ" (1).

2 Peter and Jude

These two writings demand being viewed together because a large segment of Jude is close to identical with 2 Peter's mid-section (Jude 4-19 and 2 Pet. 2:1-3:3). Those who deny Simon Peter the authorship of this short letter do so partly on the ground that a major apostle and eyewitness to Christ would not be likely to copy material from a lesser church leader such as Jude. The question becomes, would it seem more likely for the poor to borrow from the rich, or the rich from the poor? In other words, would Simon, the big fisherman, who shared so many months with Jesus of Nazareth, need to copy so much material from Jude?

The answer appears to me to be found in comparing the so-called identical passages, matching closely the verb tense. The Petrine material is in the future tense, predicting what shall be in the future. Jude's material is sent as a tract to the churches calling their attention to the fact that what had been foretold by Peter (and also by Paul) was presently coming to pass. Peter prophesied, "There *will* be false teachers among you. They *will* secretly introduce destructive heresies. . . . Many *will* follow their shameful ways and *will* bring the way of truth into disrepute. . . . These teachers *will* exploit you" (2:1-3). Peter continues his foretelling into Chapter 3 asserting that "in the last days scoffers *will* come. . . . They *will* say," etc. (3:3-4). Jude, on the other hand, upon seeing the fulfillment, reminds the believers, "Remember what the apostles of our Lord Jesus Christ foretold" (17) and he speaks of the "men whose condemnation was written about long ago" (4). One writer tells of what is yet to come. The other points to what is already present.

With Peter and Paul now martyred and James, Jude's elder brother, also killed, Jude considers it his duty to call the apostolic forewarning to mind. With Peter's death in A.D. 64, Paul's in 67 and James' in 66, I reckon the date of Jude's letter at 67 and Peter's at 60. Both of them are written from Jerusalem.

A possible objection to this theory is the line in 2 Peter, "This is now my second letter to you" (3:1). This reference to a "second letter" poses no more a problem than that posited in the letter we have been calling 1 Corinthians with its sentence, "I have written to you in my letter not to associate with sexually immoral people" (5:9). It is to human beings we owe the Epistles' names "1 Corinthians" or "2 Peter." The longer of the two Corinthian letters and of the two Petrine epistles is titled "First" and the shorter called "Second," whether that was the chronological order or not.

Since our major interest in this study is the *why* question, rather than the *where* or *when* queries, let us be content to admit the final word is yet to be spoken on time and place. It is simply my best opinion that Peter writes his prediction while still laboring out of Jerusalem and Jude gives the follow-up some six or seven years later.

As to content, Peter calls on his readers to consider the precious promises of God (Chapter 1), the false promises of men (Chapter 2) and the certain promises of Christ's return (Chapter 3). Jude, after a brief introduction honoring "the faith that was once for all entrusted to the saints" (verses 1-4), asks his readers to abhor the apostate teaching (verses 5-16), but adhere to the apostolic teaching (verses 17-23).

Jude would like to have written on the high theme of "the salvation we share" (3), but is constrained by circumstances rather to call for rallying behind the apostolic gospel in the face of substitute messages that alter essential facts and change original doctrines. This is what all heresies have tended to do.

Nothing challenges the worldwide spread of the church more than splinter groups dividing the churches and substituting the life-saving truths of Apostolic Christianity with highly polished and glittering philosophies emptied of words like "sin," "repentance" or "atonement" and leaving out truths regarding the incarnation, the cross or the resurrection. Truth implies the opposite of falsehood. Persons at every time must distinguish between religious truth and spiritual error. What the apostles of Jesus taught "once for all" is to be the norm against which all religious ideas and practices are to be measured by the congregations.

Once again the missionary concern for persons, brought to the simple gospel of salvation in Christ, is that they remain in that faith. Even the teaching on the coming day of the Lord is not to satisfy the illicit curiosity of date-setters, but to appeal for "holy and godly lives" describing "what kind of people [believers] ought to be" (2 Pet. 3:11). Transformed men and women are the strongest appeals that can be made to people considering the claims of the gospel. Right living, right teaching and right practice on the Church's part, lead to right decisions on the world's part. It is only as believers add to their initial faith qualities, like "self-control, perseverance and . . . godliness," that they will be kept "from being ineffective and unproductive" (2 Pet. 1:8).

1 Peter

Unlike 2 Peter, 1 Peter has Silvanus as amanuensis, or letter carrier, and Gentile believers as recipients (1:18; 2:10). We are led to ask why the apostle to the circumcision is writing to predominantly Gentile congregations established under Paul's influence? The theory that seems likely to me is that, at the same time Paul is preparing for his Spain mission and has turned the care of his Crete congregations to Titus and his Asian churches to Timothy, he has requested Peter (at this time in Rome) to keep an eye on the work in "Pontus, Galatia, Cappadocia, Asia and Bithynia" (1:1). If such is the case, the time is A.D. 64 when the Neronian persecution is on the horizon and the place is Rome, which in common symbolic parlance is called "Babylon" (5:13), because of its captivity mentality toward the church. The order used in mentioning the five Roman Provinces to which this encyclical is addressed suggests the route the original missionaries to the area must have followed starting from some seaport in Pontus.

The letter sees the task of every member doing all in his or her power to spread the gospel to others. Consistent lives are necessary, if the world is to listen to the gospel claims. Holiness in character precedes evangelism in power. The nudge of the apostle to the readers of his circular letter is to "live such good lives among the pagans . . . they may see your good deeds and glorify God" (2:12). That will require Christian citizens to "submit . . . for the Lord's sake to every authority" and will call for even Christian slaves to "submit . . . to masters" (2:13, 15). And, as strange as it may seem to twentieth and twenty-first century ears, "Wives, in the same way [are to] be submissive to . . . husbands" (3:1). Freedom from slavery must come and wife abuse must be overcome, but on the priority list of changes needed, the top of the list has to remain conversion of citizens, masters and husbands. So Peter explains why voluntary and temporary submission is high on God's list. Evangelism is the answer, writes Peter in the words, "so that, if any of them do not believe the word, they may be won over without words by the behavior of their wives" (3:1).

Why was it "Christ died for sins once for all, the righteous for the unrighteous?" The only possible answer for undergoing such pain and injustice is "to bring you to God" (3:18). Why is it believers are asked to put missionary evangelism before their personal rights? Why are they to "live the rest of . . . [their] earthly life . . . for the will of God" (4:2)? Social betterment that is lasting cannot occur without better persons. Salvation precedes and produces the better world for which all long. Christ has turned the world's standards upside down. His followers are no longer, like the world, to look out for self. Rather "each one should use whatever gift he has received to serve others" (4:10).

The church has different objectives than the world. We

have been called "out of darkness into his [God's] wonderful light." We who before had "not received mercy, . . . now . . . have received mercy" (2:9-10). Some scholars, seeing so much baptismal imagery in this letter, have named it a baptismal homily. The ordinance of baptism does symbolize the radical change of life and purpose expected of each immersed believer. Pagan neighbors are not only to see the baptism, they are to witness the outstanding difference in life from the convert's pagan way of acting prior to the burial in water to the change that follows. From baptism on, at which time Christ was acknowledged as Lord, the new man in Christ is "always [to] be prepared to give an answer to everyone who asks . . . the reason for the hope" (3:15) that he has.

The recipients of the letter are termed the "elect . . . who have been chosen according to the foreknowledge of God the Father, through the sanctifying work of the Spirit, for obedience to Jesus Christ and sprinkling by his blood" (1:1-2). These are to anticipate hopefully (Chapter 1), walk righteously (Chapter 2), suffer willingly (Chapter 3), think clearly (Chapter 4) and support helpfully (Chapter 5).

1, 2 and 3 John

Near the end of the first Christian century (around A.D. 95 and in Ephesus if the historian Irenaeus is to be trusted), the Apostle John is compelled, by the laxity of the second generation church and the rise of the threatening heresy which will come to be known as Gnosticism, to write the homily we call 1 John. The purpose of the letter in John's own words is "so that you may know that you have eternal life" (5:13). John uses the very word basic to Gnosticism: "know" (Greek *gnosis*). Original believers were content to walk by faith, trusting the testimony of the apostles as to that which they "heard," had "seen" and "touched" (1:1). The heretical sect was luring believers from the secondhand experiences of apostles who had walked and talked with Jesus to personal, spiritual, firsthand experiences that gave special knowledge of divine mysteries.

John knows that what might sound so good was seductive and Christ denying. Their teaching rejected the incarnation, blood atonement and bodily resurrection. The seemingly high claims to fellowship with God were belied by their "walk in the darkness" (1:6), even while denying that they were sinners.

John would give assurance of salvation to anyone who passed the three tests he lays down. There was the moral test, the social test and the theological test. A true Christian is moral and will be found to "walk in the light, as he [God] is in the light" (1:7). He will love his brothers and there will be "nothing in him to make him stumble" (2:11), like causing division by breaking off proselytes into a sectarian clique. The social test asks for brotherly love not to be violated by splitting off brothers and sisters from the one body to which they had belonged since their conversion. Theologically all true Christians hold to the central truths of God's incarnation in the person of Jesus, celebrated at Christmas; and to that key event of Christ's resurrection from the grave remembered especially at the season men call Easter. A church without faith, hope and love cannot be considered a church, but must be recognized as heresy.

Intolerance by John, like his apostolic peers, to doctrinal and moral defection, is understood, when it becomes evident that if Gnosticism lives Christianity is gone. A compromise gospel, with no cross and resurrection — no Son of God and no deliverance from sin — is no good news at all, but a fatal deception. Like every heresy since Gnosticism, the proponents start with Bible terms but so modify the meanings that the saving truth of the original message is traded for an empty theosophy that buries the truth under a deluge of empty slogans.

Truth is demanding. Error is less exacting. The gospel is based in history. Falsehood is founded on religious speculation. The true God of Scripture is "Light" (1:5), "Life" (2:25) and "Love" (4:8). When believers walk in light, manifest life and live by love, missionary work can continue apace. When forgiven people forgive each other and get along well, the church is the place outsiders long to be. Such a condition is when the populace is ready to listen to the story of Christ who is "the atoning sacrifice for our sins, and not only for ours but also for the sins of the whole world" (2:2). It is then the church can preach, without embarrassment, "We have seen and testify that the Father has sent his Son to be the Savior of the world" (4:14).

Second John is 1 John in miniature. It also points to the three tests for knowing who are genuinely saved. We see the moral test at verse 4 in the reference to "walking in the truth," the social test at verses 5 and 6 in the command to "walk in love" and the theological test at verses 7-11 pointing to Jesus' "coming in the flesh." He who sincerely accepts the story of Jesus in the New Testament records must not in the name of religious toleration "welcome" proponents of error, for in such open acceptance, one "shares in his wicked work" (11). To "continue in the teaching of Christ" (9) is the only acceptable option to one who meant it when he or she received the Jesus of history and faith as "Lord."

Third John has as its basic issue not so much doctrine as authority. Where 2 John was to be a defense against heresy, 3 John is a protecting wall against schism. A false teacher by the name of Diotrophes, "who loves to be first" (9), pits himself against the aged apostle and those workers he sends out. Both 2 and 3 John are private letters to close friends in the gospel. The latter is addressed to Gaius, a mission supporter. The comment, that "for the sake of the Name . . . they went out, receiving no help from the pagans" (7), shows how important it is that believers back the financial needs of the missionaries so no one in the field to be evangelized draw the false conclusion of the church's interest in their money rather than their souls.

Hospitality for traveling evangelists in a world with no economic Motel 6 is a commended virtue for Christians who wish to share in the "work together for the truth" (8). This may be the meaning behind the suggestion in Hebrews 13:2 that believers "not forget to entertain strangers, for by so doing some people have entertained angels without knowing it." The word "angel," translated, means "messenger." Add two letters at the beginning and three at the end and you have ev*angel*ist. The meaning may be that when Christians practice hospitality giving a room or a meal to a traveling brother, it might be that the person helped, unknown to them, was a gospel proclaimer. Such traveling evangelists, or missionaries, are ever in need of such encouraging backing in their work.

PART FOUR

The Revelation as
Missionary *Struggles*

CHAPTER 16

Missionary Struggles
With Church Weakness
Revelation 1-3

Each Gospel ended with some form of the great commission, calling on us to "make disciples" (Matt. 28:19), "preach the good news to all creation" (Mark 16:15), begin preaching "in his name to all nations" (Luke 24:47) and "feed" the sheep (John 21:17). The book of Acts traced the apostles' understanding of, and carrying out of, their Lord's marching orders. The epistles also have reflected each writer's concern for the church to stay at their assignment of reaching both Jew and Gentile for Christ. The unique book that concludes the New Testament is very different in style, but not at all in purpose, from the rest.

It is the Apostle John's intent to keep the churches at Christ's mission in the face of government threats and religious opposition. Where the Lord of the church had called for telling the story of redemption everywhere, the self-styled lord of the Roman empire had made illicit the preaching of Christ anywhere.

Domitian, who reigned over Rome's domain from A.D. 81-96, in the last year of that reign, was demanding that he be worshiped as "Lord and God." The earlier localized persecution of Christians under Nero was nothing compared to the extensive suffering brought against the church by Domitian. John's personal crime, that placed him in exile on the island of Patmos, was the evil (?) of preaching "the word of God and [bearing] the testimony of Jesus" (1:9).

Who will the churches obey? Will it be Jesus, who asks for preaching, or will it be Domitian, who calls the Christians to silence regarding the gospel? The question has become again, "Do we obey God or men?" (cp. Acts 5:29). The magnificent apocalypse, symbolizing the struggle of churches in reaching "men for God from every tribe and language and people and nation" (5:9), in the face of opposition from every quarter, calls on the readers to stay in the battle for the souls of men. The command "not to speak or teach at all in the name of Jesus" (Acts 4:18) is the will of the dragon and his helper beasts. But, the unchanging order of God is conversions everywhere. The symbolic book of Revelation, that pictures the struggle between those attempting to evangelize the world and the powers that oppose it, ends with the missionary-heart still beating strong: "The Spirit and the bride say, 'Come!' And let him who hears say, 'Come!' Whosoever is thirsty, let him come; and whoever wishes, let him take the free gift of the water of life" (22:17).

John is the author (1:4). The island of Patmos is the place of writing (1:9). A.D. 96 is the likely date. Apocalyptic symbolism is the style. But, evangelism, or world missions, is the purpose. Enemies need to be warned and believers need to be comforted; but, most of all, Christ's great and final order to win the world is neither to be forgotten nor laid aside because of the hardships it may bring.

As if writing in code, so the material could get by the military censors and on to the congregations, John paints word-pictures and uses symbols to convey the hard struggle, but certain victory ahead, for the cause of Christ. With masterful stroke he describes seven churches (Chapters 1-3), a seven sealed book of the future (Chapters 4-8), the sounding of seven trumpets (Chapters 8-11), the viewing of seven pageants (Chapters 11-14), the outpouring of seven vials (Chapters 15-16), the painting of seven symbols (Chapters 17-19) and the previewing of seven pictures of the end (Chapters 19-22).

Before we meet the enemy of the mission ("the great dragon . . . the old serpent . . . the Devil and Satan" [12:9]) and the beastly forces of opposing governments and opposing religions, it is time we meet the unexpected enemy, which is the church itself. As Peter one time had stated, "It is time for judgment to begin with the family of God" (1 Pet. 4:17). Sometimes in Christian history the failure to extend the gospel to new climes cannot be blamed upon outside interference but on inside failure. Our struggle, which is at some locales and occasions with anti-Christian governmental or religious forces, is often a wrestling with church weaknesses. Christ is perfect and the gospel is infallible, but the believers, under some circumstances, manifest weaknesses. They fail to be the winning force they were meant to be.

The Church's Purpose

It is to be noted early that John's picture of the local church is that of a "lampstand" (1:20). Its reason for existence is to let the light of the gospel shine forth from it. The purpose of a candle, or lamp, is to drive out the darkness. Be the blackness iniquity or ignorance, the church has the mission of bringing the light of the world to the people living in the darkness. It is to give its light "to everyone in the house" or community (Matt. 5:14-15).

Every congregation is to be a fellowship of concerned people for the reaching of the lost. It is the nature of light to shine. It is the place of a lamp to remove darkness, so people can see where they are going or can read messages addressed to them.

Because of the symbolic nature of apocalyptic writings and the importance of numbers in that *genre* of literature, John speaks of "seven lampstands" as "seven churches" (1:20). There were more than seven literal congregations in the Province of Asia, but the number seven will stand for all congregations at all times of history. "Seven" was the symbol of totality. Seven days constituted a full week and seven lamps stood for all congregations. The entire book of Revelation will be divided into seven scenes with seven acts composing each scene. There will be seven beatitudes in the book, dragons and beasts with seven heads, seven letters, seven trumpets, seven vials and the list goes on.

Instead of these churches named standing for the seven periods of church history, they represent the types of congregations one is apt to find in any and all times of the church. However it is that you understand the teaching of the seven letters, do not miss the way John describes the mission of each congregation. Its purpose is to uphold the light and let it reflect far and wide. Churches are "lampstands" and "stars are the angels of the seven churches" (1:20). The word "angel" is often translated in your Bible, rather than Anglicized. The word means messenger. The letters were addressed to the messengers of the congregations, who would be reading the epistles from Christ to their gathered flocks. "Lampstand" for church and "star" for messenger, turns the mind to evanglization. Stars guide ships in the night and lamps enable people to see their way in the darkness.

The Church's Problem

Although Christ envisions his congregations as lamps and their preachers as stars, the light in too many places is about to go out. Visualize a candelabrum with seven arms with wicks burning by the supply of oil provided. Two of the flames (Sardis and Laodicea) are in a dreadful state. The lights from two are in the best condition (Smyrna and Philadelphia). The state of three others (Ephesus, Pergamum, and Thyatira) are half and half — just so so. In your town, or in any place there are churches, there is apt to be at any given time some congregations very strong, some about to die out and others just getting by. The great commission struggles to be fulfilled at any given period of time, because not every church is living up to its full potential as a winning force.

Each of the letters Jesus dictates to John for his flocks to hear, contain the information of what is right with that church, what is wrong, what is needed and what is promised upon repentance. Two of the congregations are in bad shape. Sardis appeared to be alive, but was spiritually dead and did not know it. The congregation received strong condemnation (3:1). The Laodicean church had grown "lukewarm" (3:16) at its task. That condition, unchanged, would leave but a grave-marker where once lived a thriving congregation. Growing cold or suffering the blahs leads to spiritual death.

How opposite are the Smyrna and Philadelphia bodies of believers. Suffering at Smyrna kept it pure and evangelizing at Philadelphia brought positive results. Remaining "faithful, even to the point of death" (2:10), or walking through "an open door" for evangelism that God has provided (3:8), pleases the Lord and impacts the world.

Ephesus, which had enjoyed long apostolic ministries by Paul and John has forsaken its "first love" (2:4). It seems to be almost a pattern that, when believers find the initial joy of sins forgiven, the prime drive of life to them is to share their new-found Savior with others. The Ephesian church had lost this love they had at "first." If the members "do not repent and do the things [they] . . . did at first," the church will be removed. Past glories, of souls won in days long ago, will not guarantee a congregation's future. Each generation must continue the evangelistic outreach.

To tolerate the false teaching and immoral living of a Jezebel in the pulpit, as at Thyatira (2:20); or to be so broad-minded as to accept every shade of error, as at Pergamum (2:14); is to put the great commission in reverse gear, closing churches rather than establishing new ones. Robert Calvin Guy addresses our eclectic age that is embarrassed at the claim of Christ for the exclusive place as "ruler of the kings of the earth" (1:5). He writes, "He [Jesus] said, 'Decide!' — we must not say, 'Discuss.' He said, 'Follow!' — we must not say 'Compare.'"[1]

The frightening fact is that the recipients of the seven letters in Revelation, were ready to get a second opinion from the diagnosis given by the Great Physician. He saw most of them about to die. They considered themselves in pretty good shape. A trip to modern Turkey and finding Moslem mosques where in Century One were Christian churches, shows Jesus' analysis was the correct one.

The Church's Partner

Each letter's call for repentance, accompanied by an inspiring promise, was intended to motivate better results. When "the seven churches" (1:11) are first mentioned, John tells that "among the lampstands was someone 'like a son of man'" (1:13) and describes a person that can be no less than Jesus Christ. Had not the giver of the great commission promised to be with his church as they carried out his wishes, stating, "Surely I am with you always, to the very end of the age" (Matt. 28:20)? And is not that the scene in Revelation, as the curtain is pulled back to reveal the reality? The church, in the "suffering" that comes with extending the "kingdom" 1:9), is not alone, dependent only on its human resources. The Promiser, true to his pledge, is "among the lampstands." He who gives the order to witness, enables the spokesmen to carry out his command.

Seven times the commendations, condemnations and promises are accompanied by the counsel, "He who has an ear, let him hear what the Spirit says to the churches" (2:7). No warning or promise is for a single congregation alone to

---

[1]Robert Calvin Guy, "Theological Foundations." In *Church Growth and Christian Mission*, Donald McGavran, editor (New York: Harper and Row, 1965), p. 50.

hear, but is for all the churches. "The paradise of God" (2:7), "the crown of life" (2:10) or a "white stone" (2:17) ought to be all the motivation needed. "The morning star" (2:28) with its promise of a new day, or the certain hope of being acknowledged before Christ's "Father and his angels" (3:5), should lift up our drooping hands. To be "a pillar in the temple of . . . God" (3:12), or to "sit down" with Jesus on "his throne" (3:21) is intended to get our feet to marching and our lips to talking for God.

We know that history repeats itself. The church that is not a missionary church becomes in time a missing church. "He who has an ear" — even one ear — had better be listening. "The Spirit" is talking "to the churches." John is only writing down what Jesus is telling him to write. Stop, look and listen. The one speaking to us is described in seven ways (1:14-16). His "head and hair" are white, speaking of his antiquity. His "eyes . . . like blazing fire," reveal his omniscience. His "feet . . . like bronze glowing in a furnace," tell of his omnipotence. His "voice . . . like the sound of rushing waters" lets us know the power of his word. His "hand" holding the "seven stars," is to inform us that his workers are in his protective care. His "mouth" holds the "double-edged sword," pointing us to his teaching which can save or destroy and his "face . . . like the sun shining in all its brilliance" is to remind us of the glorious God we serve.

Jesus not only has "all authority" (Matt. 28:18) to command, but all sufficiency to meet the needs of every Christian soldier entering the battle to win souls for him. Language and cultural barriers in the work of missions can be overcome. The hardest fence to get over is that constructed by some church people who let prejudice limit their labors to a few of their own kind nearby.

In the year 1830, a Baptist denomination divided over the question whether the church should do missionary work or whether, if God wanted to save the heathen, He could be trusted to do it without the church's help. The 100,000

Baptists divided equally into 50,000 Primitive Baptists, leaving evangelism to God; and the 50,000 Missionary Baptists, becoming partners with God in the task. A century later there were less than 46,000 of the first group left, while the others had swollen their numbers to over nine million.

Reading the first three chapters of Revelation should have made clear to every reader that the church's purpose is missions, the church's problem is the failure to evangelize and the church's partner is Christ, who stands ready, willing and able to help any member or congregation ready to join him in the greatest work in the world.

CHAPTER 17

Missionary Struggles With Governmental and Religious Opposition
Revelation 4-18

We are admonished at various times to steer clear of discussing either politics or religion, if we would avoid controversy. John the Revelator is not one to follow that counsel, for his interest is the advancement of the church's gospel. And it is both politics and religion that will prove to be Satan's chosen partners to hinder the church in its world-encompassing mission.

Both politics and religion are forces that can count for either evil or good. So, in the wrong hands, and turned to anti-Christ goals, they can cause little but anguish for the people of God.

Religion *per se* cannot be labeled as an evil, for James speaks: "Religion that God our Father accepts as pure and faultless is this" (James 1:27). He then describes true religion as balanced between social concern for the needy and personal holiness for one's own life. Our English word "Religion" is from the Latin *religare* and refers to binding back together something that had been torn away. In a Christian context the term is quite applicable, for the Bible sees man separated from God by sin, but restored back to fellowship with Him by the atonement of Christ.

Politics, or human government, like religion, is a potential good, in that Paul could see even the Roman emperor, "God's servant" (Rom. 13:4). Without social structures, there would only be chaos with each individual doing what was right in his own eyes.

Yet, while law and order are meant for society's well-being, like game rules and referees are intended to make a sporting game fair and enjoyable, a player taking a pay-off, or an umpire tilting the game for one side's benefit, turns what was meant to be a good into an evil. So it turned out in John's time. Where Roman law had benefitted the Christian mission in Paul's earlier days, because of its commitment to fairness and justice; under Domitian, the Roman power had become a tool of Satan to block Christ's work at every turn.

Political Opposition

In Revelation 12 we meet "an enormous red dragon with seven heads and ten horns" (12:3). John leaves no question that he is talking about the "ancient serpent called the devil, or Satan, who leads the whole world astray" (12:9). The dragon's enormity reveals his threatening power and his red color suggests the spilled blood of those he seeks to destroy. His long-standing enmity against God's Son is to be continued against Christ's church.

Chapter 13 reveals the two beastly powers that will serve the dragon in his attempts to keep Christ's followers from fulfilling their evangelistic mission to reach the world.

The first beast represents human governments that ally themselves to Satan's anti-Christian goals. John's readers, being disciples of Christ and acquainted with the apocalyptic writings in the Old Testament, will see John's reference to Roman power directed against believers. In the book of Daniel the Old Covenant prophet had spoken of "four great beasts" arising "out of the sea" (Dan. 7:3), threatening God's Israel. Wild and ferocious beasts, such as lions, bears, leopards and worse, stood for inhumane governments that would arise causing harm to the people of God. When John interprets "the seven heads" in a later chapter as "seven hills" (17:9), the reference to Rome "the city of seven hills" cannot be missed.

The inhumanity of man to man is hard to believe, but it seems to continue into our present century. How beast-like can human beings become in the white heat of prejudicial hatred? Some would call it ethnic cleansing. Some would justify what is obviously bestial in the name of some perceived good, accepting the lie that the end justifies the means.

In A.D. 96 the Emperor Domitian wants no challenge to his supremacy. He insists on every citizen burning incense to him, acknowledging him alone as "Lord and God." The Christian tenet of monotheism, with believers ready to pray for the state but not consider it the highest power, was bound to bring an inevitable clash. John could be said to be writing God's version of Gibbon's *Decline and Fall of the Roman Empire*, as seal after seal is broken revealing more of the previously closed book of the future. By pictures of horsemen pre-shadowing victory, then civil strife, then famine, then pestilence, followed by martyrdom and falling stars, Rome's downfall is assured and the church's victory promised (Chapters 6-7).

Readers of the Apocalypse are wise enough to see that Rome's opposition to Christ, leading to her defeat, is but a pledge that other later powers of history, choosing the same anti-church stance, would come to a similar end. History does repeat itself. But over all the centuries in which God allows the church to apply its efforts to win the lost, no political entity will be capable of stopping Christ. He is Lord of history.

When the final history book is written, it will tell of persons "purchased . . . for God from every tribe and language and people and nation" (5:9) and it will report the redeemed as "a great multitude that no one could count" (7:9). That record of happenings on earth will not fail to tell of efforts by atheists, Communists and Nazis, thinking they had buried once for all what they liked to call the "superstition" of Bible believers. Yet, as surely as the crucified Christ became the living Christ again, the Bible, thought to be entombed in antiquity, lives again with God's order, "You must prophecy again about many peoples, nations, languages and kings" (10:11). Church history could not read otherwise, for it tells of "the eternal gospel" which God intended to be proclaimed "to those who live on the earth — to every nation, tribe, language and people" (14:6). Let all Christians sing to the Father and the Lamb, "All nations will come and worship before you" (15:4). Let every congregation foresee the end of all the hard battles for Jesus in the scene John paints: "The kingdom of the world has become the kingdom of our Lord and of his Christ, and he will reign forever and forever" (11:15).

Religious Opposition

The second beast, arising to assist the Devil in his efforts to drown out the church with propaganda against her, is a religious entity (13:11-18). This anti-Christian power will be called "the false prophet" and one who "performed miraculous signs" (19:20). The beast hid its true nature by putting on the appearance of "a lamb," but blew his cover to anyone listening carefully, for "he spoke like a dragon" (13:11).

Church and State join forces in their efforts to destroy the Christian cause. Pagan governments gain power over their citizenry by creating a State religion which calls for giving one's very life for the political entity's cause. John words this phenomenon: "He exercised all the authority of the first beast on his behalf, and made the earth and its inhabitants worship the first beast" (13:12).

The beast was expert in deceiving "the inhabitants of the earth" (13:14). He was able to deny jobs to believers and bring death to anyone refusing to go along. John says this *religio-politico* entity marks its subjects, as surely as Christ seals his. The number tattooed on hand and forehead is said to be "man's number" and to be "666."

This is not the number of some particular human — the number of *a* man — such as rises in most every generation, having a name whose numerical value of letters adds up to 666. From Nero to the pope to Stalin, the figuring has had to be strained to appear to support each theory. The number 666 is said rather to be "man's number." If seven stands for perfection, six falls short of perfection. The triune perfection of heaven's Father, Son and Spirit is 777. The utopias that human leaders promise to build always fall short of their loudly-shouted assurances. Listen to the electioneer's promise of a human paradise upon receiving the votes of the populace. Stand back and count how many campaign promises are broken, as the rosy vision of better days, once again, fades into the midnight of disappointment. Man always falls short. The best he can do is 666.

"Right hand" and "forehead" are the proper places for the mark of the beast — the sites on the body where Jews wore their phylacteries. Hand and head stand for action and thinking. You can tell a Christian for his mind thinks as Christ teaches and his hands do the work the Lord wants done. A servant of the Dragon thinks and acts like the Devil.

Do you know a modern missionary whose work is opposed by Hindus in India, Moslems in Iran or Jews in Israel? It is sometimes hard to tell if the opponent to the gospel is a government or a religion, they are so closely wedded. When today an evangelical believer goes to work for Christ in a South American country or an Eastern European state, the visa refusal can be said to be a political decision, yet the suspicion remains that the emphasis ought to be placed on the State-*Church* rather than the *State*-Church.

Christ's people have had two thousand years to get used to these facts, so clearly stated by John. Satan has married politics and religion into an unbreakable union that will not allow for the freedom to preach Christ's gospel without compromise. If Paul had to escape over the wall in a basket, or John serve time on an island in the sea reserved for criminals, it is important that the future of our cause be revealed. Christians are on the winning side. Human governments rise and fall. God's kingdom will know no end. Satan has a lot of power, as he "prowls around like a roaring lion looking for someone to devour" (1 Pet. 5:8). But be encouraged, the Lamb will conquer the lion! The voice from heaven loudly shouts: "They overcame him by the blood of the Lamb and by the word of their testimony; they did not love their lives so much as to shrink from death" (12:11).

CHAPTER 18

Missionary Struggles Overcome
Revelation 19-22

You may remember the scene at a pet shop where the father asks his little daughter which of the small puppies in the window she wants. If you recall the incident, you will not have forgotten her answer. Looking at the friendly one right before her, who was wagging his tail for all he was worth, she said to her daddy, "I want the one with the happy ending."

The book that closes our Bible — "The revelation of Jesus Christ" (1:1) — is a happy ending, indeed. While it pictures in livid color the realities of hardship the churches must face in their assignment to let the world know about Jesus, it also paints in bright hues the wonderful state of glory awaiting all who have shared in the venture. Throughout the book are scattered glimpses of the rewards that lie ahead for Christ's partners in the mission. But nowhere are the scenes more wondrous than in the final chapters. How can one reserve a place at heaven's banquet table? How can a person be sure to share in the "wedding of the Lamb" (19:7)? How is the reservation made to guarantee housing in the New Jerusalem or acreage by "the river of the water of life" (22:1)? John gives at least one answer in each of the final four chapters.

Follow the Rider on the White Horse (19:11-16)

The horse in Bible days was an animal used in war. An ass was the beast of burden to carry loads, but the horse was the steed for conflict. At the end of the battle the conqueror would mount "a white horse" as the symbol of victory. John's dramatic scene in Revelation 19 is a picture of Christ's cause winning in the end.

That Jesus is the rider on the horse is clear by his names "Faithful and True" (19:11), "the Word of God" (19:13) and "KING OF KINGS AND LORD OF LORDS" (19:16). How faithful has Christ been to his promise, "I am with you always, to the very end of the age" (Matt. 28:20)! How true to his word, "You will receive power when the Holy Spirit comes on you; and you will be my witnesses" (Acts 1:8)! Here in the Apocalypse, as in his Gospel and First Epistle, John titles Jesus "the Word of God" or the one through whom the Father has expressed His will most clearly. No one else could be considered for even a moment as the King over all kings. His penetrating "eyes" show his omniscience and the many diadems placed on his head (19:12) point to him alone as worthy of all worship.

The main point John is making is that the victory has been won by the "sharp sword" of his mouth (19:15). It could not be more plain that the teaching of Jesus is powerful. That weapon to which triumph is attributed was earlier called "a sharp double-edged sword" able to cut both ways. It could save or destroy. It could bring deliverance to friends and destruction to enemies.

We must not overlook "the armies of heaven [that] were following him, riding on white horses and dressed in fine linen, white and clean" (19:14). This host who shared in the battle, now shares in the victory, also riding on white horses. White horses stand for winning the fray, but what is the meaning of white linen? The answer does not call for guesswork. John writes the intent of the symbol, saying "Fine linen, bright and clean . . . stands for the righteous acts of the saints" (19:8).

Standing back and looking at this mural John has painted, one sees through picture-language a church marching into the battle for souls around the world. The weapon of that warfare is Christ's word. The leader going before us into the field of conflict is Jesus. Whenever the church, God's army, is dressed in white (i.e., doing "righteous acts"), the evangelism battles are won. That is the same lesson found in the epistles, as they called for holy living in order that "the teaching about God our Savior [be] attractive" (Titus 2:10). The gospel of Christ is the sword of the Spirit. It wins battles when held in holy hands.

Help Bind the Dragon (20:1-6)

The "angel," or messenger, that "seized the dragon . . . or Satan, and bound him" with a great chain "to keep him from deceiving the nations anymore" (20:1-3), may refer to the church. At least Paul looked to the Devil's defeat by Christ's working through his people. He wrote, "The God of peace will soon crush Satan under your feet" (Rom. 16:20). When the church goes to marching, entering the battle against evil, Christ gains the victory and defeats the enemy under the marching feet of his army.

We sing, "Christ has no hands but our hands to do his work today, he has no feet but our feet to guide men in the way." As we sing, we remember that the work of Christ is carried on by the people in whom he dwells. We also recall that Satan's plans come into fruition through the persons he has made his subjects. Those addicted to drugs or tobacco got started by the work of a pusher or a highly-skilled adverᵗiser who could make deadly poison look attractive. Win to Christ a prostitute or a pimp and one of Satan's workers becomes a worker for God. Each convert from the ways of sin to the way of Christ and the Devil's hands are tied. No longer will a force for darkness be turning a neighborhood bad, since that force through the gospel has been turned into a power for good. Evangelism, once again, has been shown to be God's strategy for social change.

At the burial in the waters of baptism of a former enemy of the church (as in the case of Saul of Tarsus), there rises from that liquid grave a new life to work for the kingdom's advancement. That process of turning Satan's workers into servants of Christ is the way of binding the soul's enemy for "the thousand years," or long time, of the church age. For the church age is the gospel age, when the Holy Spirit is bringing new birth and freedom from the ancient serpent.

The day will come when the deceiver will be "thrown into the lake of burning sulfur" (20:10). But until that final day of Christ's return, the Satanic deception can be controlled by locking up the evil one through the powerful chain of gospel proclamation.

Fill up the Holy City (21:1-22:5)

As Jesus said before, there is lots of room in heaven. You can't invite so many persons to join you there, that some will be kept out for lack of space. John earlier had cited Jesus saying, "In my Father's house are many rooms" (John 14:2). Now again, the Apostle describes the tremendous size and magnificent beauty of the "new Jerusalem, coming down out of heaven from God, prepared as a bride beautifully dressed for her husband" (21:2).

Everything about heaven is appealing: As beautiful as was the garden of Eden in Genesis before the fall of man, is Paradise restored at the end according to Revelation. The land where death, pain and mourning will be no more, ought to be the destination planned for every son of Adam. The locale where cowardice, unbelief and immorality cannot coexist should be the final home for all daughters of Eve.

Precious gems, shining with the glory of God, predict heaven's happiness. High walls assure its protection from harm. Solid foundations speak of its endurance. "Gates on the east . . . north . . . south and . . . west" (21:13), tell anyone with eyes to see that from whatever part of earth he or she comes, open doors invite entrance. Will only lowly peasants from Galilee respond to heaven's kind invitation to walk in that city where "God gives . . . light" (21:23)? Far otherwise! "Nations will walk by its light, and the kings of earth will bring their splendor into it . . . the glory and honor of the nations will be brought into it" (21:24,26).

The one requirement is that reservations be made in advance, for "only those whose names are written in the Lamb's book of life" (21:27) may enter. Skin color or national origin is not what is looked for on your visa, for the water of life and tree of life is "for the healing of the nations" (22:2). But be advised, no "impure . . . shameful or deceitful practice" (21:27) will make it through customs. Let every sinner know how welcome he is to come to Christ, but level with him or her that, while there is plenty room for the individual, there is no room for his pet sins. Christ's "I do not condemn you. . . . Go now and leave your life of sin" (John 8:11) is the unchanging way to the eternal city. Give out the invitation to all you meet. But don't try to lower the price or change the requirements.

Use the Little Time Remaining

Martin Luther once said, "The Bible is alive, it speaks to me; it has feet, it runs after me; it has hands, it lays hold on me." I am affected by the Scripture in the same way. In these last pages of Revelation, I hear the giver of the great commission speaking to me in the imagery there, "Follow the rider on the white horse into the battle for the hearts of men. Help bind the Devil by converting his workers into laborers for the Lord. Fill up the holy city by enlisting every soul you can for the future world where Christ reigns. And use the little time remaining by giving priority to Jesus' last command."

Three times in the final verses of Revelation Jesus gives the assurance, "Behold, I am coming soon!" (22:7,12) or "Yes, I am coming soon" (22:20), as if to tell either readers or hearers we don't have forever to win the lost. Life in the new heaven and earth will be forever, but our lives on earth are but for a short span. Of all the wonderful things to do in the next life, soul winning will not be one of them. That joy of evangelizing is for this life alone. Everyone in the holy city will have already been redeemed.

It is from the giving of the commission to the Second Coming of Christ, that saving the lost is our high privilege. How much time remains before Christ returns, or how many months or days you and I will have to reach another for salvation before we are invited to the next world, no human is privileged to know. But, for every remaining time period of life on earth, the Holy Spirit in partnership with the church works for the redeeming of fallen persons. "The Spirit and the bride say, 'Come!'" and the hearers of the good news offer the broadest of all invitations to "whoever wishes" (22:17).

Time may be shorter than we have imagined. Paul B. Smith titles his first chapter "Not Maybe but Must," catching the urgency in Christ's voice as he tells his disciples their mission to "go into all the world and preach the good news" (Mark 16:15).[1] M.D. Babcock rightly observes that a believer who has "no interest in missions betrays either a woeful ignorance or a willful disobedience."

The Lord, who is "coming soon," will "give to everyone according to what he has done" (22:12). As I close the covers of this final revelation from Jesus to me and to you, I must

---

[1]Paul B. Smith, *World Conquest* (London: Marshall, Morgan and Scott, 1960).

ask the penetrating question of "what" I have "done" about the assignment from Christ to his followers. If judgment was based on what I have thought, or have written, or have even preached, my conscience could be more comfortable. Even looking at my records of confessions of faith taken and persons baptized, filling pages of a personal diary, does not bring total satisfaction, because there are yet so many more that need to hear. He is coming soon. The heart's response, "Amen. Come, Lord Jesus" (22:20) is modified by the unspoken prayer, "but give me a little more time to bring some more people with me to glory."

Conclusion

"Faith [does] come by hearing" (Rom. 10:17). May action also come by hearing. The word of God from start to finish is clear that God wants the lost saved. It is further definitive that the world's hearing of such divine love is dependent upon the Christians accepting their place as intermediaries between God and humankind.

The Gospels bring into focus the one who would be Savior to any sinner willing to trust in him. The Acts relates instance after instance of lives changed, after hearing the testimony of a believer and responding in the public acknowledgment of that faith, being baptized. The Letters from different inspired penmen to various persons and churches keep the witness of the believers effective by holding them to holy living and apostolic faith, lest the communication be muffled. The Revelation pulls back the curtain to reveal the church struggling with multiple forces attempting to squelch its saving efforts, yet succeeding in turning eyes and hearts to heaven's king. All these twenty-seven books of the New Testament were written over approximately fifty years of time, but were meant to be guide for the Christians throughout every period of the church age.

As you read and reread your New Testament, let "he who has an ear to hear" (Rev. 2:7), listen for purpose. Why did God inspire the New Testament writers? Why did He see that those writings be preserved for us to read? He wants everyone of us to know His will for the lost's redemption! He seeks for each of us to make His purpose our purpose. Throughout the millennia God has never changed his mind about the mission. The purpose of a channel is to carry the water of life to those who famish without it. Harold Lindsell[1] calls on the church not to see itself as a reservoir to hold the water of life but as only a channel through which it is to flow.

You know enough Bible to save the world. Let it flow! Do not dam it up for future use at Bible studies to be enjoyed by the saved. Let it flow! Let it flow to the arid souls about you thirsting for but a drop of hope or a cup of forgiveness. The purpose of God — the purpose of the church — the purpose of the New Testament — is to save those outside. Don't keep it. Give it out to "whoever is thirsty" (Rev. 22:17). Today would be a perfect time to start.

---

[1]Harold Lindsell, *Missionary Principles and Practice* (Westwood, NJ: Fleming H. Revell Company, 1955), p. 40.

Bibliography

The Abingdon Bible Commentary. New York: The Abingdon Press, 1929.

Paul G. Alley. *The Missionary Enterprise.* Unit VII. Wheaton: Evangelical Teacher Training Association, 1962.

Anderson, Bernhard W., Editor. *The Books of the Bible II: The Apocrypha and The New Testament* New York: Charles Scribner's Sons, 1989.

Bliss, E.M. *The Missionary Enterprise.* New York: Fleming H. Revell, 1908.

Bonhoeffer, Dietrich. *Letters and Papers from Prison.* New York: Macmillan, 1953.

Carson, D.A. "The Purpose of the Fourth Gospel: John 20:31 Reconsidered." *Society of Biblical Literature,* Volume 106, Number 4 December, 1987.

Carter, William Owen. *Why They Wrote the New Testament.* Nashville: Convention Press, 1946.

Carver, W.O. *Missions in the Plan of the Ages.* Nashville: Broadman Press, 1951.

Choate, J. C. *Missionary Preparation.* Winona, MS: J. C. Choate Publications, n.d.

Cook, Harold R. *An Introduction to the Study of Christian Missions.* Chicago: Moody Press, 1954.

Eusebius. *Ecclesiastical History.* Grand Rapids: Baker, 1974.

Filson, Floyd V. *Opening the New Testament.* Nashville: The Westminster Press, 1952.

Grant, Frederick C. *The Gospels: Their Origin and Their Growth.* New York: Octagon Books, 1983.

Guthrie, Donald. *The Pauline Epistles: New Testament Introduction.* Chicago: InterVarsity Press, 1961.

Guy, Robert Calvin, "Theological Foundations." In Donald McGavran, Ed. *Church Growth and Christian Mission.* New York: Harper and Row, 1965.

Lindsell, Harold. *Missionary Principles and Practice.* Westwood, NJ: Fleming H. Revell Company, 1955.

Marshall, I. Howard. Luke: Historian and Thologian. Grand Rapids: Zondervan, 1970.

Martin, Ralph. *New Testament Foundations: A Guide for Christian Students,* Volume 1. Grand Rapids: Eerdmans, 1975.

McCasland, S. Vernon. "New Testament Times" in *The Interpreter's Bible Volume VII.* New York: Abingdon, 1951.

McGavran, Donald A. *Understanding Church Growth.* Grand Rapids: Eerdmans, 1970.

McLean, Archibald. *Where the Book Speaks: Mission Studies in the Bible.* New York: Fleming H. Revell, 1907.

Morgan, Carl H. *The Layman's Introduction to the New Testament.* Valley Forge: The Judson Press, 1968.

Moule, C.F.D. *The Birth of the New Testament.* New York: Harper and Row, Publishers, 1962.

O'Neill, J.C. *The Theology of Acts in Its Historical Setting.* London: SPCK, 1970.

Ong, Walter J. "Text As Interpretation: Mark and After" in *Semia,* 39. Decatur, GA: Scholars Press, 1987.

Smith, Paul B. *World Conquest.* London: Marshall, Morgan and Scott, 1960.

Stott, John R. "The Great Commission" in Carl F. H. Henry and W. Stanley Mooneyham, Editors, *One Race, One Gospel, One Task,* Volume I. Minneapolis: World Wide Publications, 1967.

Strachan, R.H. "The Gospel on the New Testament" in *The Interpreter's Bible,* Vol. VII. New York: Abingdon, 1951.

About the Author

Alger M. Fitch currently resides in Turner, Oregon with his wife, Betty Jean. Dr. Fitch has taught teachers to teach and preachers to preach for over 55 years, and has traveled in as many countries. He has ministered to various congregations in the Northwest since 1940 and has taught at Pacific Christian College since 1968. As a modern day Apostle Paul he has invested his energies in writing, teaching, and visiting mission fields! His mission travels throughout Europe have been under the auspices of Toronto Christian Mission; South Seas Christian Ministries has sponsored his preaching to the islands of the South Pacific.

Alger received the B.Th. from Northwest Christian College, B.D. from Phillips University, M.A. from the University of Southern California, and Rel.D. from the School of Theology at Claremont. Some of his published works include *Claiming God's Promises*; *Revelation*; *Afterglow of the Resurrection*; *Alexander Campbell: Reformer of Preaching and Preacher of Reform*; *Best of All Is Jesus*; *Preaching Christ*; *What the Bible Says About Money*; *What the Bible Says About Preaching*; *One Father, One Family*; and *Pick the Brighter Tulip*. He has authored numerous articles for the *Christian Standard* and has lectured at countless events. Alger's writings reveal his undying passion for world evangelism and the efforts at uniting Christ's church.

The Fitches have two daughters, Luana and Marcia, and a son, David.